SPIDER
PREACHER
MAN

Books also by Paula Montgomery:

The Hazel Weston Series

Canyon Girl

Valley Girl

Hood River Girl

In Grandma's Footsteps

The Becka Bailey Series

Coyotes in the Wind

Down the River Road

A Summer to Grow On

When November Comes

Because of Patty

(Out of Print)

SPIDER PREACHER MAN

From Motorcycle Gangs to God

PAULA MONTGOMERY

WESTBOW°
PRESS
A DIVISION OF THOMAS NELSON
& ZONDERVAN

The Twelve Steps are reprinted with permission of Alcoholics Anonymous
World Services, Inc. (AAWS). Permission to reprint the Twelve Steps does not
mean that AAWS has reviewed or approved the contents of this publication or
that AAWS necessarily agrees with the views expressed herein. AA is a program
of recovery from alcoholism only. Use of the Twelve Steps in connection with
programs and activities which are patterned after AA but which address other
problems, or in any other non-AA context, does not imply otherwise.

WestBow Press books may be ordered through booksellers or by contacting:

WestBow Press
A Division of Thomas Nelson & Zondervan
1663 Liberty Drive
Bloomington, IN 47403
www.westbowpress.com
1 (866) 928-1240

Scriptures taken from the Holy Bible, New International Version®, NIV®.
Copyright © 1973, 1978, 1984, 2011 by Biblica, Inc.™ Used by permission of
Zondervan. All rights reserved worldwide. www.zondervan.com, The "NIV"
and "New International Version" are trademarks registered in the United
States Patent and Trademark Office by Biblica, Inc.™ All rights reserved.

ISBN: 978-1-4908-2956-2 (sc)
ISBN: 978-1-4908-2957-9 (hc)
ISBN: 978-1-4908-2955-5 (e)
Library of Congress Control Number: 2014904631

Printed in the United States of America.

WestBow Press rev. date: 03/27/2014

In memory of
my high school English teacher,
Ada B. Poole,
who inspired me
with her inquisitive spirit
and self-sacrificing devotion
to her students
and their education

He has sent Me to heal the brokenhearted,

To proclaim liberty to the captives,

And the opening of the prison to those who are bound.

—Isaiah 61:1b (NIV)

CONTENTS

Chapter 1

BEFORE THE SNAKEWEED BLOOMED

Coyotes yipped and yowled, stretching their necks to the rising moon that silvered the sands of eastern Arizona. Then their voices quieted, leaving the Indian reservation to sleep in the pale light. But a harsh sound shattered the stillness: the coarse, drunken voice of a father arriving home late; a father venting his anger, his frustration, on a small child.

"I told you to shut up!" slurred the giant. At least he looked like a giant to five-year-old Spider Montero* who cowered in a corner, steeling himself against the next blow. He sucked in his breath and tried not to cry, but a whimper escaped.

---

* To respect the "anonymous" in Alcoholics Anonymous, a pseudonym has been used.

Crash! A stool hit the floor as a calloused hand struck the young head. "Stop that noise, you little brat!"

Something seared through the child's ear, and a warm, sticky stream oozed out and trickled down his neck. Welts from the blows began to swell along the thin arms and ribs, making the boy's body throb painfully.

The noise had awakened the baby, Magdalena, and now her squalling added to the commotion. Spider's older sister, Mary Ann, must have hidden somewhere, because she was nowhere in sight.

The boy cringed as he watched his father's arm poise to strike again. *¿Por qué, Papá?* (Why, Father?) Why had this gentle man turned into such a monster? This man whose very step the child copied whenever they roamed the hills and arroyos together.

Suddenly, a shadow crossed between boy and father, and Spider saw his grandmother's long, gray braids dance at her back when she declared, "No more! You hit me—not the boy!"

The man's stony face crumpled, as if the old woman's fist had struck it dead center. But no more fists or voices would rage that horrible night. The last sound the child heard as he folded to the floor was that of his father's boots shuffling out the door.

The next days blurred in blackness. The boy remembered little except the pain when he would rouse to drink herbs his grandfather had brewed for him. Once in a while, his mother's soft voice would filter through nightmares with messages like, "That wasn't your father, *niñito*. That was the drink demon."

An image wove in and out of Spider's dreams: the image of his short, plump grandmother guarding him from angry, flailing arms. Her words were like a medicine man's magic, making the arms vanish in an instant.

Her words ... Somewhere in the boy's tender mind he understood their power, because among his people, words were rarely spoken between a woman and her son-in-law. He understood much more in the twilight place between sleep and pain, where he saw his proud father trying to prove himself a good provider when jobs were scarce in the bleak land. And no matter how gracious the grandparents, simply their presence was a constant barb to Henry Montero, reminding him of his failure. In his own way, the boy understood those things, but the Apache part of him kept that insight quiet. The Hispanic part, however, longed to confide in someone. He wanted to share his real feelings with a person who would understand. The closest he came to that kind of sharing was with his Grandfather Joe. But the old Yaqui's reserved nature often intruded on their talk.

As Spider healed and was able to return with Mary Ann to school, he noticed that when he clapped a hand over his right ear, he heard little through his left ear: no trills of a bird, no thumping of a rabbit. From then on, the boy learned to turn the right side of his head toward sounds, just as a doe twitches her ears to the slightest noise.

Spider Henry Montero had been born the summer of 1943 on the San Carlos Apache Indian Reservation in Arizona. With the absence of his father at the time, his grandfather, Joe Luque, had named the boy. Joe had surveyed the hairy, skinny arms and legs and tiny potbelly, musing awhile before deciding the baby resembled a spider, thus naming him accordingly. And to keep peace in the family, Joe added "Henry" for the boy's father, Henry Gonzales Montero.

Spider's twin brother didn't make it through the ordeal of birth and neither would nine other children born to Frances Montero. Out of seventeen babies, only seven would survive the rigors of childbirth: first, on the primitive reservation, and then later, in a different kind of primitive setting—a California ghetto.

The bruises faded from the small body, but the memories stubbornly lingered.

"Grandfather," Spider asked as he raced after the old man, "when will my *papá* come home?"

"I do not know, *niñito*."

They ran together every morning, tall Joe Luque, with his long, straight gray-black hair flagging behind him, and the grandson, whose dark curls flopped around his tanned face. His eyes, always eager, searched for wildlife or for some unexpected treasure. That morning, his treasure was the sun rising above distant hills, bringing the desert floor to life with a blaze of spring color: the brilliant yellows of wild marigolds, mesquite blooms, and senna against the deeper shades of sorrel. Owl clover added a sprinkling of violet-pink to the design on nature's loom. As Spider ran, he could already smell the senna's rich fragrance filling the air.

"Do you think my father will come back?" he called, his voice breathless as he began to lag behind. The short legs couldn't stay astride of the man for too long.

"Yes, he will come back." Joe Luque sounded confident and not the least bit winded. "Shame may keep him away many weeks—months maybe—but love for you, your sisters, and your mother will swallow shame and bring him back."

Spider considered the statement for some time before asking one last question, "Will he still drink beer and wine, Grandfather?"

The old man grunted and then slowed, allowing the youngster to catch up. "I think he will. There's something inside him that wants to drink."

They turned and headed back to the house. Unexpectedly, a jackrabbit sprang from its hiding place, delighting the boy who watched its velvety black tail seesaw toward another thicket.

"But your father won't hurt you again," Joe Luque promised. "And till he comes home, I take care of you."

The man kept his word, teaching Spider and his cousins, Roberto and Louie, how to track animals, hunt and fish, and find water in the desert. Their grandmother also helped with the education, passing on age-old Apache instructions in her native tongue, "Look after yourselves while you are alone. If you see a thick bunch of trees or bushes in front of you, don't go into it," she warned. "There might be a mountain lion or other wild animal in there, waiting to attack you. Always go on the upper side or the lower side of such a place."

The boys nodded in awe, realizing they had just heard advice that had first been bestowed many generations before.

Besides survival techniques, Grandfather Joe taught the youngsters how to skin animals and craft things from the inedible portions. Not one part of an animal was wasted. Even from the bones, they crafted trinkets to sell. And Joe Luque himself had made the sharp knives they used, each knife fashioned to the hand of its young owner.

Spider never tired of watching the skillful old craftsman etch pictures in leather and silver, bringing the plain material to life with graceful wild horses or clumsy bears splashing across some river in an unknown place. The boy would imagine himself there, far from the reservation's parched ground of summer.

The nearby stream, from which they fetched water, still ran freely enough. But Spider had heard about another tribe, the White Mountain Apaches, who were blessed with high lands; wide, cool rivers; and tall trees to shade them from Arizona's merciless sun.

Instead of a tree, Grandfather's ramada outside the house shaded him from that sun while he worked. Withered vines climbed up the four posts and crisscrossed overhead on a trellis of sticks. Oftentimes, travelers stopped at the ramada and examined the Indian's knives, leatherwork, and jewelry on display. Although quiet and gentle by nature, Grandfather Joe was a shrewd businessman and managed to get top prices for his wares.

"What do you do with all the money you make?" Spider asked one day after a sale.

"Most I save," the man replied, "because someday I buy a real house for your grandmother and me."

"What kind of house, Grandfather?"

"A house with water pipes inside, with lights you turn on at walls."

"Oooh!" The boy was transfixed by the thought. Then he frowned. "But, Grandfather, there are no houses like that around here."

"No, but fine houses there are in California where some of our people live. I save money for one of them fine houses."

Spider didn't like the idea of his grandparents moving so far away, and he told the man so.

The older face nearly crinkled into a smile. "Maybe you come to California, too." And that thought excited Spider's imaginings even more.

Magdalena had shed her cradleboard and was toddling everywhere now. Spider helped Mary Ann chase after the chubby little girl, keeping her safe from the snakes and scorpions that shared their land.

"Magdalena!" he would call, scooping her up and carrying her back closer to Mother, who ground corn at the doorstep. The little girl's fat cheeks would blow out giggles, making Spider laugh too. She wore the same tiny black cross on her forehead that Grandmother Luque had tattooed on the foreheads of Spider and Mary Ann years before when they had been baptized at the Catholic mission.

"That shows you are Christian now," the old woman reminded Spider more than once, "not some wild, heathen Indian. So act like a Christian!"

But how did a Christian act? Spider wondered. Most of the Sunday Mass was in Latin. Somewhere, maybe halfway between the "mumblings," the *Padre* did preach a short sermon in Spanish, which Spider understood. But his mind would often wander to the adventures awaiting him outside the church walls. Then he would fidget, bringing a sharp look from his grandmother.

"Hush!" she would warn. "Or you'll never get picked to be an altar boy." That would quiet Spider momentarily while he focused on the two, white-robed boys kneeling behind the priest. *The best part is ringing the bell*, he thought. Yes, he would like to become an altar boy—just to ring that beautiful tinkling bell!

One summer morning soon after Spider's sixth birthday, Grandfather Joe called to the boy and his cousins who had stayed overnight. "It is time for your test," the man said.

Spider straightened his back, trying to look courageous as the man guided a horse and pony toward them. First, Grandfather blindfolded each one of the boys and then helped Spider to mount. Next, his cousin Louie slipped in behind him on the same pony. Spider knew Roberto would ride behind Grandfather.

All three boys were dressed alike, in nothing but a breechcloth and moccasins. Only a sheathed knife and small water bag dangled at each side as the two horses trotted from the homeplace. Spider's mind held a picture of his mother—a picture of her stirring ashes in the adobe oven that huddled in the yard. She had glanced only briefly at him before the blindfolding, but he had caught the mixture of concern and pride in her face.

His heart beat faster with each jostle of the pony. He was worried that he might not remember everything his grandfather had taught him about survival in the desert. At least Roberto and Louie would be along, and with all three of them working together, they should be able to find their way back home in the allotted three days.

Sweat began to tickle at Spider's eyebrows, but he didn't dare touch the blindfold. Grandfather might think he was peeking, thus forfeiting the chance to prove himself a true brave. Along with Spider's Spanish heritage, the blood of four Indian nations surged through his veins: Apache, Yaqui, and, according to his mother, the ancient Maya and Aztec. The boy was eager to prove himself worthy of such ancestry.

Spider could feel the sun's warmth coming from higher overhead as the pony trotted on. First, there was the firmer dirt of the roads. Then, Grandfather must have headed them straight into the wilds where not even a trail marked the way, because Spider felt his pony's unsure footing beneath him as it climbed into hilly country.

At long last, Grandfather halted the horses, ordered the boys down, and then commanded, "You must be home by noon of three days or you not pass test. Keep eyes covered till you don't hear horses."

Because of his hearing loss, Spider was first to strip the bandanna from his face. Blinking in the bright sunshine, he gathered his bearings. A sudden loneliness gripped the boy when he spotted the silhouette of his grandfather and the horses galloping over a ridge. Spider wanted to race after the man and beg him not to leave them all alone in the desolate place. But that was not the Indian way. The boys must prove themselves and their learning.

By now, his cousins were also blinking their eyes, adjusting to the brightness. Then Louie stood and caught the last sight of the old man as he disappeared over the horizon. "Come on!" He whooped, heading that way.

But Spider and Roberto didn't follow. Instead, they searched the ground for incoming tracks and found them—in the opposite direction! Spider chuckled. "Grandfather is tricking us, turning away from home." The old man would undoubtedly circle back later.

Hollers soon persuaded Louie to return for a council. Should they find shade and rest there until the sun lowered? That would conserve their meager water supply and head off the danger of sunstroke.

"But we have only three days to reach home," Louie protested.

"And we'll have to begin looking for fuel early to build a fire," his brother added.

"And we have to trap something to cook on that fire," offered Spider, suddenly feeling grownup and important among his fellow tribesmen.

By nightfall, a fire blazed after their dinner, and Spider was more than eager to lie down in the hollow he had carved for himself in the soil. During those quiet moments, he thought of his father. What if the man were sleeping just beyond the next ridge? Or perhaps he had traveled way up into the White Mountains and was enjoying the last morsels of a trout next to a lake or river. Spider wondered: *Did his father ever think of him and the rest of the family on such nights filled with the cricket's song? Did he miss them?* Guilt welled up within the boy. He blamed himself for his father's disappearance. After all, it was shame over the beating that had driven the man away.

Even during the bleakest of moments that night, when the yelps of coyotes encircled the boys and they stoked the fire to burn brighter, Spider felt other eyes watching: soft, friendly eyes like those of his grandfather.

"Hmmm!" he mused. Was the old man tracking them, making certain they didn't run into trouble? He smiled at the thought, knowing Grandfather Joe would never admit to such a thing. But Spider was able to sleep comfortably as he imagined his grandfather on the lookout nearby. Still, the boy kept his good ear up—just in case.

When his water bag emptied, Spider used the container to hold treasures he found along the way: an arrowhead, a tooth, and a shiny black rock. The boys found the fluids they needed in a barrel cactus. But, by the third afternoon, all of them welcomed a violent thunderstorm that rolled across the desert. The three tired, dry bodies seemed to soak up the rain as they hugged the earth and lapped at puddles like gleeful puppies.

Then they lay back under the retreating storm and breathed deeply of the pungent smell of creosote bush that hung heavy in the air. Spider knew his grandfather made medicine for sores from the creosote leaves. He also knew that many grasshoppers and crickets lived in the yellow-flowered branches. But he wasn't quite hungry enough to eat the little creatures—yet.

He and his cousins sprawled lazily among the fluffgrass for another hour, watching small flocks of desert sparrows pick the ground and bushes for insects. Not one sprang the traps set for them. But a gamel's quail wasn't as lucky.

That evening, Spider drifted to sleep with the mourning dove's song, a melancholy cooing that set his thoughts on home. Tomorrow, they had to reach their destination before noon, Grandfather had said. The boy hoped with all his heart that they would make it in time.

Feeling energized, all three boys rose before dawn and started on the last stretch of their journey. Startling awake some cactus wrens, the youngsters grinned at the harsh reprimand they received. "Ka-ka-ka-ka!" the wrens scolded.

Although the rain had blotted out their tracks, they were close enough now to recognize landmarks and fairly flew toward the wonderful aroma of tortillas—real or imagined—wafting to them through the morning air.

Spider felt as if all his senses were keener now, like those of a wild animal zeroing in on its prey. But the prey was his mother's corn cakes, and he would not rest until he tasted their sweetness melting on his tongue.

Just as the sun cleared the eastern mountains, all three boys raced one another down the final road, breathlessly laughing when they collapsed at last on the back doorstep.

Mrs. Montero, cooking breakfast in the yard, greeted them with, "Wash before you eat!"

And Grandfather Joe was there, pronouncing his blessing on them, "You did good, my sons," making Spider's heart swell with satisfaction and new love for the old man.

Just as the rabbitbrush and snakeweed began to bloom that summer, an uncle arrived in a rusty truck and carried off the grandparents and all their belongings to California.

Before leaving, Grandfather Joe promised Spider that the boy and his family would follow shortly. "Your father will come soon, and he bring you all to California. There is work for him there. And I build a place for you, too."

Spider watched sadly as the truck groaned down the road, leaving the boy to brood alone. His father was coming home—and his only source of protection was driving far, far away.

CHAPTER 2

BEYOND THE GIANT SAGUAROS

Slow summer days slipped by, long and lonely without Grandfather Joe and his plump Apache wife. And although Magdalena busily shadowed her "big brudder," to the boy the house and yard still felt empty. The ramada, stripped of the old man's wares, stood bleak and shabby on the parched, beaten earth where even the air seemed too weary to stir up a dust devil.

Then one morning in that split moment before blinking awake, panic sprang upward from the pit of Spider's stomach. Heavy boots had tapped the floor near his bed, and the boy knew in an instant—*mi papá!*

Overhead, the darkly handsome face of Henry Montero grinned down on his son, while Spider quickly took in the open-collared shirt tucked into belted jeans; the muscular, tawny arms; and the slicked-back hair, every strand in place.

Still grinning, the man asked, "So, what have you been doing with yourself?" as if he had been gone only a short while.

The boy's breath caught in his throat, but he managed, "R-Roberto, Louie, and me, we spent three days in the desert and got back in t-time."

"That's good," the father said, his roughened hand gently touching the smaller arm, the closest thing to an apology proud Henry Montero would ever give his son. "Now, do you want to help me fetch water?"

Spider leaped up, wriggled into his jeans, and scurried after the man. Only the clanking of their buckets made noise on the way to the stream. But the silence between the twosome was companionable, and the boy sensed that his father was sorry for the beating of long ago. At the same time, the self-blame Spider had carried as surely as the water buckets suddenly dropped away, leaving him feeling lighthearted. He smiled much that day.

Mother had built the morning fire, and Spider could smell her corn cakes frying as he set down the bucket. He watched her look shy, then almost playful as she vied for her husband's attention. At breakfast, the parents talked of California and of the house that Grandfather Joe had bought on the outskirts of Los Angeles.

"My father says there are many jobs for you in the city. He says he has built his garage into a nice little house for us—if we want to go there."

Henry Montero gazed around him at the blistered land, then at his three children quietly munching their cakes. "Hmmm!" was his only reply.

But the following week, the same battered truck that had carried away the grandparents now carted off Spider, his family, and everything they owned. Sandwiched in back between a mattress and table, Spider stared solemnly at their empty house, the withered ramada, and the oven still smoking in the yard. His uncle and aunt were there with Roberto and Louie, lined up like four clay sculptures squinting against the sun.

Allowing only one tear to escape, Spider turned and poked his head up into the breeze, avoiding the dust cloud that churned up from the road. Once the truck lumbered onto a paved highway, the miles unfolded quickly, eventually bringing them to the fringes of Phoenix. There, they bought gasoline and lingered awhile in a nearby parking lot. Mary Ann and Spider watched Magdalena while the older people took a brief *siesta* in the truck.

Although everything had turned brick-hot under the broiling sun, the children found some grass on which the little sister could play without blistering her bare feet. Heat waves were rising from asphalt and concrete, blurring the buildings around them. After *siesta* time, they all climbed back aboard the truck and left the sprawling city behind.

Later, as the vehicle groaned up a road that wound gently into some desolate hills, Spider stared, enchanted by the giant saguaro cacti stretching their prickly round arms to the sky. For miles, they stood at attention against muted desert colors, and Spider thought he could never tire of watching them. The boy's imagination ran wild with the hot wind that whipped furiously at his curls. Some of the cacti looked ancient; a little stooped and scarred, like old warriors after too many battles. Some resembled athletic young braves, strong and perfectly formed. And some were small, revering the older ones who formed protective clusters about them.

The boy recalled Grandfather Joe telling him once about the saguaro, how the wind "sang" through the spiny arms—if a person was very quiet and listened closely. Spider strained his good ear for the saguaro's song but heard only the whir of the tires and drone of the engine.

At night, they camped along the roadside while moonbeams bathed the desolate sand and sage in a haunting silence. The next day, mile after sunlit mile skimmed past as the truck meandered toward the California coast. When it finally neared the sea, Spider's nose twitched like a young coyote testing the wind. The air felt cooler as a fresh, briny smell reached his nostrils.

Suddenly, after the road lifted and dipped, Spider beheld the ocean for the first time in his six years of life. He gasped at the shimmering vast blue that stretched to the sky's edge. And the shoreline seemed alive, waves rolling, splashing, then creeping flat across the sand.

It didn't take long for all three of the children to land on the ground and head for the beach. Sharing a stale corn cake with begging gulls, Spider studied their funny, arrow-shaped prints in the wet sand. Those prints gave him an idea. Soon he had found a piece of driftwood, then a shell, to fashion an Indian village at the water's edge while Mary Ann chased waves and the grownups napped.

Magdalena clapped her pudgy hands together in delight while her "brudder" created little hovels, roads, and mesas near her brown feet. She squealed with pleasure and tried to copy him. Something in her rapt, sweet face caused him to sculpt bigger and bigger houses, even cows and horses—*anything to make Magdalena smile*, he mused.

Then through the enchanting sounds of the surf, he heard his mother's voice urging the children back to the truck, back to the road. The seascape disappeared, along with its fresh scent, which was soon replaced by the pungent odor of oil and stagnant water. Buildings came into view. Then the truck jerked to the right and headed into a more populated area.

They passed boxy-looking houses in soft pastel colors, side by side, with square yards filled with tanned children and an occasional barking dog. Then the houses began to look tattered, the children much darker, many of them black-skinned, and Spider spied only one dog, which seemed undernourished and listless in the late afternoon sunlight.

The truck traveled on, through an ugly sprawl of factories and warehouses, then on to a commercial area where sad storefronts along littered sidewalks stared back at him. Spider shut his eyes. He felt trapped in a cluttered new world, a forest of buildings and people. And he felt himself longing for the open spaces of the reservation or even for the seashore—not here, not where everything seemed to smother him and his family.

Spider quickly forgot those feelings, though, when at long last the truck pulled into the driveway of a clay-colored house. Out he jumped and raced straight for the open door. "Grandfather!" he called.

In moments, he was hugging the tall, straight Yaqui and his Apache wife, while the faintest of smiles revealed their pleasure. Spider noted that the old man's silvering hair was still long and looked freshly washed.

The others pleasantly filled the kitchen while Grandmother puttered about and served up bowls of hot, steaming beans with crisp tortillas. After an orange for dessert, Spider marveled at the electric lights and then wandered through the few rooms, discovering the bathroom.

"Does our place have a toilet, too?" he asked his grandfather.

"Uh-huh!" came the guttural reply, bringing a wide smile to the boy's face. *No more outhouses!*

The entire family was then escorted across the back yard to the garage that had been made into their new home. Although it was small, to Spider it looked like a palace. Grandfather Joe had put up room dividers, so there were two bedrooms, a small living room, a kitchen, and a tiny bathroom.

Mary Ann raced to the kitchen faucet and turned it on— just to watch the water run out. At dusk, more relatives arrived to help carry in furniture. And long after darkness had snuffed out day, Spider climbed into his own bed and closed his tired eyes. Magdalena had fallen asleep hours before; now she was snuggled next to Mary Ann in their bed across from him.

At dawn, Spider could almost feel the pulse of the city quicken as it—and the boy—began to wake up. He drew on his clothes, wedged his feet into his cramped shoes, and then headed across the lawn to where his grandfather was stretching his long, lean legs before his customary morning run. Then man and grandson set out along the broad street. As before on the reservation, the boy began to lag farther and farther behind. But here, Grandfather Joe had to stop at street corners if there were any cars, and those pauses gave Spider the chance to catch up. On and on they jogged, while the youngster gaped at the various early risers, mostly Negro and Hispanic, who emerged from stairwells and front doors. He would later discover other nationalities in his Watts neighborhood as well, such as Filipino, Chinese, Japanese—and even American Indian like himself. He spotted very few white faces as he continued to run.

"That's your school," his grandfather pointed out as they raced past a brick building and fenced-in playground.

Spider's heart thumped a little harder as he thought about the new school and the adventures awaiting him there. Turning back, the two retraced their steps, passing the same storefronts and houses as before. The traffic began to thicken as the sun peeked over warehouses to the east. The city seemed fully awake now.

Later that day, Grandmother took Spider's hand and marched him down to the *barrio* where a little Spanish Catholic church fought for space on a street corner. "This is where you'll go to church with us tomorrow," she said. "And we will ask the priest about catechism."

"Cat-ay-what?"

"Catechism," she explained. "You need to study your catechism so you can make your first Holy Communion and then learn to become an altar boy."

"And ring the bell?"

"*Si!* And ring the bell."

Thus began Spider's religious training. Once a week, he joined other Spanish-speaking boys and girls in catechism class, reciting the memorization his mother had helped him with.

The elderly priest, Father Morton, asked Spider in Spanish, "What is the seventh commandment of God?"

Spider stood up and carefully replied, "The seventh commandment of God is: Thou shalt not steal."

"Gracias!" The priest smiled at Spider, then asked the girl beside him, "What are we commanded by the seventh commandment?"

"Uh," she began, "by the seventh commandment we are commanded to respect what belongs to others ... uh ... respect what belongs to others," she repeated.

Father Morton smiled again and finished the sentence for her, "to live up to our business agreements, and to pay our just debts." He chuckled. "You're too young yet to worry about business and debts. But someday, you might be working at a job. Then you'll need to pay back loans and pay taxes, like your parents do now."

"But, Father," came a voice from across the circle, "my old man lost his job and he don't got no money to pay back his loan, and some guys came and beat him up."

The priest sobered. "I'm sorry to hear that, son. Maybe there's some way I can help."

Spider liked Father Morton. Although he was white, the priest reminded him of Grandfather Joe—old, wise, and kind. The child did his best to please Father Morton by faithfully studying his lesson each week.

Almost immediately upon their arrival, Henry Montero found a job at a laundry company. And just before school began, he took Spider to a department store and bought him new clothes and shoes.

Spider felt proud of his freshly starched trousers and shirt as he walked with neighbor boys several blocks to the brick building that had come to life again after a long summer's rest. It was there on that first day, among so many different nationalities, that Spider first heard the ugly term, "half-breed." Some boys, obviously Mexican-Americans, spat the term at the newcomer through lips curled in scorn. Because Spider didn't understand the term, he simply ignored them.

As soon as he reached home, however, he asked his grandfather, "What is a half-breed?"

"Well, I would say, you are a half-breed, *muchacho*. Your father's people are from Mexico and your mother is Indian— Yaqui and Apache."

Spider tilted his head. "So I am half Mexican and half Indian?"

The old man nodded.

"Is that bad?"

"No, that's good. You come from good people on both sides, good people who make good things, who know many stories of their peoples—good peoples," Grandfather Joe repeated.

His words left the boy confused. If being a half-breed was good, then why were the boys at school hurling the term at him like a weapon? Well, he would show them. He would study hard and prove to them all that half-breeds were, indeed, good people.

Magdalena, who had heard his voice, was tugging at his pant leg. "Brudder! Bring candy?"

Spider shook his head. "No, baby! No candy today. I have no money." The boy went out the door and crossed over to the garage-made-into-a-house to change out of his good clothes. He would spend the rest of the afternoon playing ball with his little sister.

The months rolled on, and Spider was finally ready to make his first Holy Communion. Family members, who had moved to the Los Angeles area, came to the little church in the barrio that day and watched Spider take part in the ceremony. His dark skin contrasted with the white shorts and shirt he wore. At his neck hung a neat white tie that his grandmother had knotted for him. After the special Mass, various aunts, uncles, and cousins all crowded into and around the grandparents' house for a feast.

The rooms, scented with sweet aromas from the kitchen, echoed with talk and laughter while Spider sat in the midst of everyone and tried to look important.

Not too long after that special day, Magdalena awaited her "brudder" after school, as usual. "Mamma has money for candy," she hinted.

"That's nice," Spider said as he headed for the bedroom. After changing clothes, he spied his mother's purse on the couch. "Where is Mamma?" he asked the little girl, whose yawn and rumpled pink dress told him she had just awakened from a nap.

"I dunno," she said.

"Hmmm!" Spider's mind was churning. He loved buying sweets for his small sister, who was always so appreciative. His mother's purse still sat on the couch, taunting him. A moment's shame pulsed through the boy as he remembered his catechism lesson, *The seventh commandment of God is: Thou shalt not steal*. But those lovely laughing eyes were pleading with him.

Ignoring his conscience, Spider snapped open the purse and pulled a quarter from inside. "You stay here!" he ordered Magdalena. "I'll be back soon with some jelly beans just for you."

"Ooooh!" The girl squealed in delight as Spider swiftly crossed the yard and headed down the street.

Minutes later, while he paid a clerk at the neighborhood grocery, the boy heard tires squealing against asphalt, then a crashing sound outside. People began to run past the window, and with a sense of uneasiness, Spider grabbed the bag of jelly beans and followed after them.

With mounting alarm, the boy squeezed through the crowd until he spied the front end of a truck smashed against a power pole. Spider's senses spun wildly when he spotted a familiar pink dress behind one of the tires. There lay the small crumpled body of his sister.

"Magdalena?" he asked weakly. Then his voice began to tremble with anger. "Magdalena! Get up! Mamma will be mad that you followed me." He held out the brown paper bag to her. "Magdalena?"

A deep voice came from somewhere overhead. "Is she your sister, young man?"

"*Si!*"

"I'm sorry, boy," the voice said. "Your sister is dead."

Chapter 3

BARRIO BEGINNINGS

At first, there was only numbness. Then nothing could ease the pain that filled the boy. Spider felt as though he were carrying a heavy stone inside his small chest. Even on the brightest of days, his world looked dark. Lively little Magdalena was gone. Never again would he feel her tug at his pant leg or hear her sweet "brudder" begging for attention.

During the funeral, Spider had run off and hid in an alley, waiting until long after the houses emptied of relatives. Then he slipped unnoticed back to his room.

But the room turned on him. The sight of Mary Ann's sleeping face, streaked with dried tears, stabbed anew at his heart. Too many things reminded him of Magdalena—her doll, her tiny moccasins, and even the empty place where she had always slept in the crook of her older sister's arm.

Spider blamed himself for her death. "If I hadn't stolen that quarter from Mom's purse, Magdalena would still be here." She had followed him to the store and had run out into the street, straight into the path of a truck. The image of her crumpled body flashed again and again to his mind, preventing sleep.

But no matter how tired Spider acted in the mornings, Grandfather Joe still took a duty upon himself by walking the boy and his sister to school. Then the old Indian would cross the avenue and begin his daily jog, dodging harried passersby as if they were merely tumbleweed rolling through some vast open desert.

One such morning, after Mary Ann had left them on the school steps, the man finally spoke of the family's grief. "I know the sadness inside you, boy. Your mother, she don't talk—just looks, but don't see. Your father, he drinks much again. Goes to bars after work and comes home late every night. You don't sleep. Mary Ann, she cries all the time." The voice was gentle, caring. "But the bad hurt inside you will go away. You must think of new things. You must play with your friends—run, throw ball! That will chase away the hurt."

"Yes, Grandfather," Spider replied respectfully, never daring to confess that it was he who had led the little girl to her death.

Because of the circumstances, Grandmother didn't force Spider to attend catechism, and the lessons were left unstudied. After about three weeks, however, she clasped the boy's hand one late Saturday afternoon and led him to the barrio church again, this time pushing him up the steps. "You go to confession!" she ordered. "Then maybe you sleep." She left him there facing the huge door.

Spider felt embarrassed, but obeyed her by entering the darkened church. A few people stood in line, waiting near the confessional. The boy took his place behind them, watching candles flicker before a statue of the Sacred Heart. Shifting from one foot to the other, Spider silently practiced what he would say to Father Morton. He came close to fleeing several times, but decided to go ahead and follow his grandmother's advice.

At last his turn came, and he crept into the confessional box. Kneeling, the boy made the sign of the cross and said, "Bless me, Father, for I have sinned, and my last confession was a month ago."

In the darkness, he could make out the shape of the old priest through the grate. "And my sins are ..." The boy hesitated and then blurted, "I stole a quarter from my mother's purse, and I killed my sister!"

There was a gasp from the other side of the grate, then, "What do you mean, my son?"

Spider found it hard to whisper past the lump in his throat. "I-I mean, because I stole the money, God punished me by taking my sister."

The priest's quiet voice was soothing. "No, no, my son! God doesn't kill innocent little children. That was an unfortunate accident, but not your fault. You mustn't blame Him or yourself."

Slow warm tears gathered in the boy's eyes and then spilled over. "Are you saying God wasn't punishing me for stealing?"

"Oh, He is certainly displeased with your sin. And you can pray three *Our Fathers* as penance for that. But, my son, trust me—God did not take your sister's life in order to teach you a lesson."

"Yes, Father!"

"Now, pray a good *Act of Contrition*, and don't forget to say your penance before you leave the church."

Nodding, Spider began the prayer, "Oh, my God, I am heartily sorry for having offended Thee …"

When he pushed open the church door later, Spider left the heavy weight of guilt behind him. He went out into the clear evening where loiterers smoked, joked, and gambled openly along the sidewalks. But the boy didn't notice the ugliness there. He saw only a cool, fresh evening where dusk seemed vivid with color, and he heard only the sweet music of church bells tolling. Even his father's drunken insults later didn't disturb the boy. And just as Grandmother had predicted, he was finally able to sleep—all night long.

Spider resumed catechism, and then he began special classes until he had memorized all the altar-boy responses.

His grandmother looked proud the day Spider followed Father Morton to the altar. Dressed in a white surplice over a black cassock, the boy knelt carefully at his place beside the treasured bell. He felt nervous but didn't make one mistake during the Mass.

The beginning of his career as an altar boy, however, marked the ending of Father Morton's tenure at the barrio church. The priest was sent to Africa, which Spider considered nothing short of exile. And the new priest, a Mexican-American, wasn't as tolerant as his predecessor. In fact, the new priest lacked patience with mischief-makers, especially ones dressed in altar-boy vestments.

At nine years, Spider spent some of his free time playing marbles. One Saturday afternoon, his next-door neighbor, Joey, called out for him to join him in a game.

"Nah!" Spider retorted. "Maybe later. I gotta go get some stuff for my mom."

Tagging along to the grocery store, Joey asked, "Do you know that Billy's folks make booze out back of their place?"

"You don't say?"

"Yep! And we could sneak some out—easy—he says."

Spider halted a moment. "You mean Billy would help us get some?" ("Get" sounded better to him than "steal.") And he again found himself pushing aside the counsel from his catechism on the seventh commandment.

"Sure! There's so much of the stuff," Joey insisted, "no one'll miss a little." A silent struggle began between Spider and his conscience. He pictured his father's nightly ritual of staggering through the front door and passing out on the couch. The scene wasn't a glamorous one, and the boy remembered what Father Morton had preached, time and again, about the evils of drinking. But Father Morton wasn't there anymore, and Spider didn't want Joey and Billy to think he was "chicken."

With a deep breath, Spider asked, "So, what's the plan?"

That night, after the neighborhood noises had settled down, the three boys met in the back alley, then climbed the fence to the "stash" and uncorked a bottle.

Billy tried to act much older than his ten years, lifting the jug to his mouth and guzzling its contents boisterously. He smacked his lips. "Hmmm! Good! I drink this all the time," he boasted, handing it on to Joey who repeated the performance.

Next, Spider took the bottle and concentrated on masking his anxiety. His wildly beating heart would surely betray him, he thought. Up went the bottle, and the sour tasting beer slid down his throat. Although it made the boy's nose and throat burn, he didn't dare complain. Like the others, he pretended to enjoy himself.

The bottle soon emptied and a second one passed along clumsy hands. All of a sudden, Spider felt a different and massive hand, this one gripping the back of his neck. And he heard the thickened speech of Billy's father boom, "What do ya kids think yer doin'?" The man had caught them red-handed.

Without warning, he lifted Spider straight into the air and let the boy dangle there like a helpless puppet, then marched in the direction of Grandfather's house.

CHAPTER 4

POISON LIKE A RATTLESNAKE'S

Moments later, Billy's father deposited Spider at his grandparents' doorstep and barked, "You keep out of my yard, and don't come back for any reason!"

The boy's face burned with embarrassment. To worsen matters, Grandfather Joe stood in the doorway, shaking his head slowly. "I think moving from reservation would give you better life. But now I think maybe we leave better life at reservation." Saying nothing, Spider slunk across the yard to his home and bed.

The next morning, he awoke with a painful, swollen head. Still, his mother insisted he dress for church. By then she—and probably the entire neighborhood—had heard about the boys' devilry the night before.

"Ha!" she scoffed. "An altar boy with a hangover!"

Shame again warmed Spider's face, but he bore it in silence. Later, he managed to stumble through Mass without further embarrassment. Afterward, while the priest talked with parishioners, Spider and the other altar boy retreated to the sacristy, a room where vestments were kept. Removing their special garments, the boys hung them in a closet. There on a shelf sat the extra stock of communion wine in pretty glass decanters. Spider felt his mouth begin to water, and a strange sensation seemed to drive his eyes toward the bottles.

I wonder if communion wine tastes better than homemade beer, he mused. When the other boy left, Spider quickly reached for a bottle, removed the stopper, and then took a sip. Yes, it tasted better but still stung his throat and nose. Hastily, he replaced the bottle on the shelf. As he turned to leave, however, something seemed to pull him back to the closet. Confused, Spider looked numbly at the decanters. He didn't really like the wine's taste, but he felt drawn to it. Something deep inside him craved more, an empty place he had never known was there. Hurriedly unstopping the bottle, he took another swig and then raced from the room as if some invisible monster were chasing him.

Later, while kicking a can along the sidewalk home, Spider remembered what his grandfather had said once about Henry Montero's drinking habit: *There's something inside him that wants to drink.* "Is that something now inside me too?" the boy asked himself. He wasn't quite ten years old yet. Nine-year-olds didn't become alcoholics—did they?

"Nah!" he exclaimed and drove the can farther with a swift kick.

At school on Monday, when Spider met Billy, the neighbor blurted, "I showed my dad, all right! Wait till you see what's in my lunch pail." Later the boy shared the contents of his thermos—more of the homemade brew—with Spider and Joey. From then on, several times a week, Billy smuggled the forbidden concoction to school.

But Billy's offering wasn't enough for Spider. He began to sip from any leftover whiskey or beer bottles he could find at home. Also, Joey's older brother would supply the boys occasionally. In fact, one day Joey had managed to hide some full bottles of wine near the schoolyard. As soon as classes ended, the three youths hid behind some boxes in an alley and drank the wine to the last drop.

When Spider suddenly noticed the daylight fading, he tried to stand up. But a dizzying wave of nausea sent him reeling. "We'd better get home, or our moms'll de— moms'll—" His tongue refused to follow his thoughts. Again he noticed the darkness. It was descending faster than usual. His legs felt heavy. In fact, he couldn't make them move. Without warning, everything turned black. His mind swirled with worried voices and then—nothing.

The next day, Spider awoke bleary-eyed on his grandparents' couch. Grandfather Joe was holding a cup of steaming herbs under the boy's nose.

"Hmmm! Good! You wake," the old man said in his soft, quiet voice. "I think maybe you dead. Some boys die, you know. Alcohol is poison, like a rattlesnake's. It can eat up your insides and kill you."

Spider's tongue felt too swollen to answer, and his head was pounding again. After a few sips of his grandfather's medicine, the boy fell into another deep sleep.

The next time he awoke, the house was quiet. Few street noises filtered through the open windows, and darkness hovered outside. Spider turned his face toward the figure that dozed in a nearby chair. Grandfather Joe seemed shrunken in size, perhaps weighted down by worry over his wayward grandson.

As if sensing the boy's thoughts, the old eyes flicked open. Then their sad expression bore into Spider until he squirmed uncomfortably. Grandfather Joe leaned close, his voice trembling with unaccustomed emotion, "Yes, I think having water piped into house and lights turned on at walls be good for you. I think school here and people here be good for you. Your father makes money that buys you good food and good clothes. But everything has turned bad—bad!"

He pronounced the second *bad* with a profound weariness. Then leaning back, he seemed to gather enough strength to finish, "I afraid someday you become like your father. You go off, months maybe, away from family, leaving them feeling sad. Your children, they grow like you, with no father most of time."

The somber words hung in the air like some foreboding prophecy, stirring the boy's conscience. "I'll try, Grandfather," he promised. "I'll try not to drink anymore."

In that moment, the boy meant the words. But days later, as soon as Joey or Billy offered him a drink, Spider eagerly gulped it down and started the cycle all over again until he drank so much another blackout followed. Again, Grandfather Joe nursed him back to health, and again, Spider would vow not to drink. But his friends would goad him into "just one sip," and the cycle would begin anew.

Spider kept his alcohol cravings in line during the week with what his neighbors could smuggle to school or by finding something leftover in one of his father's discarded bottles. Then on Sundays, he would sneak gulps from the church's stock of communion wine.

One morning after Mass, however, the priest returned to the sacristy earlier than usual, catching Spider with a decanter fully tipped at his mouth. "What do you think you're doing?" the priest exclaimed, visibly shocked.

Any childish innocence had long since faded from the boy's face, and he felt no remorse, no respect for the man of God standing there. Calmly, Spider replaced the stopper and drew his brows into a defiant frown. "I'm surviving, Father. I'm surviving." Brushing past the priest, Spider Montero thus brought his career as an altar boy to an abrupt end.

The summer before he entered sixth grade, neighborhood teenagers who sold "joints" on the street introduced Spider to marijuana. By then, he had stopped attending church altogether, much to his grandmother's grief. Another year of drinking, smoking marijuana, and running the streets at all hours with friends, toughened the boy who had once been sensitive to the tiniest miracle of nature in a quiet desert.

In Watts, his earth was cement or asphalt. His mountains were warehouses, factories, or stores. The only animal sounds at night came from alley cats, scrounging through garbage or yowling and fighting. Even when there was a full moon over the city, Spider rarely looked up to appreciate it. His world was the street, the here and now, the drink or "joint" he could connive out of someone.

Wherever he went, "half-breed" hounded him. Short for his twelve years, Spider began to learn how to fight, how to command respect from guys much larger than he. Meanwhile, his grandparents looked on helplessly; his father continued his after-work drinking ritual; and his mother stayed busy with the babies who lived through childbirth: little Ralph, Rosario, and tiny Juanita.

Although Spider loved his brother and sisters, he kept his guard up now. Never would he allow himself to become as attached to them as he had been to Magdalena. Life was too unsure—and the pain too great when a life was snuffed out. The alcohol and marijuana helped Spider keep a stout wall around his emotions.

The first day of junior high, the boy arrived equipped with a zip gun, a knife, and a half-pint of whiskey, all stashed securely in his locker. He then made friends quickly with other students of Mexican descent. That first day, Spider drifted through classes without trouble. To his surprise, he actually enjoyed some of them—especially art class, in which the teacher, Mr. Jenkins, complimented Spider on his sketching ability. Moreover, Mr. Jenkins made a deal with the boy, "If you develop into a good artist, I'll personally buy some of your work."

Spider could feel a new sense of pride rising inside himself. Perhaps he had inherited Grandfather Joe's artistic talent. Also, he noticed, someone besides his grandfather had actually taken an interest in him, Spider Montero. He was already looking forward to his next art class the following day.

"Hey, Chico!" came a voice from behind him in the corridor. "What's going on?"

Spider turned toward the friendly black face belonging to Genie, a tall, muscular boy from his neighborhood.

"Nothing much. Art class was okay."

"Yeah, man! That Jenkins is all right."

Spider worked the combination on his locker and slipped a brown bag into his friend's hand.

Genie eyed both directions before sneaking a swig of the whiskey. "Ya wanna shoot some baskets after school?" he asked, handing the bag back to Spider who also took a sip, but not as cautiously as his friend did.

"Sure!" Spider grinned. Thus far, junior high school agreed with him.

At the cafeteria, he and Genie sat with another friend, "Little Boy," who described the various gangs in school. "They're always fightin' each other, and sometimes guys get hurt real bad." Little Boy was a half-breed like Spider, drawing them to each other in a kinship of sorts.

As afternoons at the basketball court progressed, more youths—mostly Chicanos—joined Spider and his friends. Following a game or two after school, they would all drift downtown together and crowd around a drug store table, sipping spiked soft drinks, smoking cigarettes, and joking.

The biggest joker of all was "Peanuts." He could make something funny out of the most tragic of circumstances. Another boy, whom they hadn't nicknamed yet, would reach into his pocket and bring out a fistful of marbles, then roll them around the table top for entertainment.

"These are my insurance," he explained one day, his face twisting with savage glee. "They're almost as good as brass knuckles in a fight." He scooped up a handful and clenched his fist. "Makes my punch real mean, man!" From then on, they dubbed him "Marbles."

The only one of their number who made Spider uncomfortable was Joe. Tall and lean, with a perpetual bored expression, the boys had dubbed him "Crazy Joe." He was afraid of nothing, and already his brown face bore some scars as evidence of that bravery. Early on, Spider had determined to stay on Crazy Joe's list of friends, because he suspected an enemy could end up in bad shape.

The group had grown to eight in number by the afternoon they decided upon a collective name for themselves, the "Chivaros." That was also the afternoon that their group became another gang at the junior high school. Oddly enough, they elected officers for the Chivaros in as democratic a manner as if they were gentlemanly members of the school debate club.

The Chivaros joined the bedlam at weekend football games, hurling insults—and empty bottles—at visiting teams, then adding to the fights that would erupt afterward. Girls joined the Chivaros on Saturday nights, when they would all troop into a local theater or a dance, usually stirring up things before the evening ended. Drinking and smoking pot had become commonplace to them all.

Because most of the Chivaros had been raised Catholics, one of their favorite hangouts became the CYO (Catholic Youth Organization). For the most part, they acted respectful around the priest and other adult volunteers. Although Spider was short, he was strong and quick, and could maneuver a basketball trickily through a crowd. The exercise freed him, at least momentarily, from the ever-gnawing confinement he felt. His Watts neighborhood had become prisonlike to him, the littered streets with graffiti crawling up dingy walls. In Spider's youthful mind, he saw no way out—ever.

By then, his father had purchased a television set, and the boy had glimpsed "the good life" as shown on the screen, where families sat around tables at night and really talked to each other. Where fathers came home at five o'clock and acted genuinely interested in their children's affairs.

Spider found his closest hope to that way of life in the Chivaros. He felt a bond with the other gang members, who had taken a blood oath to defend one another to the death. *After all*, he reflected, *wasn't that what real families did, defend one another?*

The only other positive influence on Spider besides the CYO club was that of Mr. Jenkins, the art teacher. Already the man had kept his promise and had bought a couple of the boy's paintings. Then, when the CYO club was invited to a Hollywood Christmas party for underprivileged youth, Mr. Jenkins found a bona fide suit for Spider to wear for the occasion.

Only a few of the other Chivaros had managed to dredge up good clothes for the event. Then, the lucky ones boarded a bus waiting at the CYO club. For one special night, Spider left his stark world behind and was dropped into a different dimension, one of glamour, rich tasting treats, and entertainment.

Jimmy Durante beamed out at him, the big-nosed singer bellowing a Christmas song in his clipped way. Then Roy Rodgers and Dale Evans, glittering in western garb, harmonized together. The sound of their voices seemed to squeeze Spider's calloused heart. Was that the way a husband and wife were really supposed to act? Singing and smiling so lovingly at each other? Spider remembered only a few glimpses like that between his mother and father—years before on the Indian reservation, right after Henry Montero had returned. Now, worn, dazed looks blotted out any affection on their faces. And Christmas, Spider knew, meant his father would have the opportunity to get drunker longer.

The memory of that special night in Hollywood remained vivid in the boy's mind the rest of his seventh-grade year. The few privileged Chivaros would recall the event again and again for the others, describing the various celebrities and their acts.

That summer, Spider found another opportunity to escape from Watts, at least temporarily. He worked alongside his mother and sisters, picking vegetables in San Bernardino Valley while the latest baby, Mary Magdalene, slept on her cradleboard nearby. At night, they bedded down on cots in crumbling shacks—if they were lucky. Otherwise, they slept on the ground and in their car.

Each morning, Spider would shiver in the chilly dawn air, his back cramped and stiff after a night on the ground. Lighting his first cigarette of the day, he would lean against a tire, pull a blanket up closer to his chin, and enjoy glimpses of the camp waking around him.

There were soft, friendly greetings among women at the water spigot as they started meals for their large families. The valley, spreading beyond in every direction, looked gray in the muted morning light. The San Bernardino Mountains overhead were sometimes smothered in banks of fog that would soon crawl heavenward like eerie spirits, then vanish, revealing the lofty range and bright, blue sky above.

Gathering buckets for his family, Spider would lead them to the fields where tomatoes peeked out among vines in neat, long rows, the vegetables looking too plump for their tight red jackets. The boy loved the scent of a new day, when the smell of damp earth and growing things swirled around the pickers. But then the sun would break through the fog, and as the fireball mounted the sky, it would begin to cook them, ever-so-slowly at first, then miserably as the afternoon wore on. And on days when smog blotted out the mountains, when the air was still and close, his mother would make them all break for a *siesta*. But then they would return to the fields and work later into the evening to make up for time lost.

Despite the hard work and primitive conditions, Spider liked the camp and the easy camaraderie there. The haunting music of the *braceros*, heartsick for their Mexican homeland, filled the night while children played tag, happy to be children again, however brief their fun.

One evening, before Spider snuck his usual drink from a concealed whiskey bottle, he wondered if he could sleep soundly enough without it. Sighing, he decided not to try, took a long draft, and then settled down for the night.

The Monteros' picking season was cut short unexpectedly when an uncle arrived with sad news. Grandfather Joe had fallen and had died shortly thereafter. Relatives from as far as New Mexico were already headed to Los Angeles for the funeral, the uncle reported.

A few days later, with a stony face and weeping heart, Spider watched as the old Indian was laid to rest. In his own quiet way, Grandfather Joe had tried to act as a substitute for Spider's real father, teaching him much. But along with love for the boy had come suffering as the man witnessed the stranglehold alcohol had on the young life.

Guilt and loneliness nearly overwhelmed Spider at the gravesite. "*Lo siento, mi abuelo,*" he whispered. How he wished he could undo all the grief he had caused his grandfather!

Spider returned to school, vowing never to allow himself to love anyone again—until he noticed a familiar face in the crowded hallways. The face was older, more mature than the young Suzanne Reves he remembered from the reservation school years before. Although she was short, her slenderness gave an allusion of tallness as he watched her long, silky black hair sway behind her.

Quickly catching up, he asked, "Suzy, is that you?"

Her look met his in frank puzzlement.

"Uh—aren't you from San Carlos Apache Indian Reservation in Arizona?"

She nodded, and only when she had turned full face toward him, revealing her large, dark eyes under a fringe of thick lashes, did Spider begin to feel his heartbeat quicken. Her face seemed perfectly shaped with high cheekbones, and her caramel-colored skin looked smooth and unblemished.

He shifted his notebook to the other side and tried to look taller and more casual. "I'm Spider Montero, remember?"

Her lips curved into a wide grin, revealing beautiful white teeth. She did remember him. "And I remember your grandfather," she said. "He made lovely silver things."

Spider felt his face suddenly go limp. Then he nodded, telling her, "My grandfather just died a few weeks ago."

"Oh, I'm sorry." Her splendid dark eyes were fixed on him as if she could read all the grief in his soul.

In that moment, tough Spider Montero felt shy. "Uh …
I'll see ya around," he said. Then he walked in a daze to his next class. *Little Suzy Reves is all grown up—into a beautiful woman!*

CHAPTER 5

AS BLACK AS THE GILA MOUNTAINS

When Spider discovered that Suzanne and her family attended the Catholic church in the barrio, his interest in Sunday Mass was suddenly revived. Grandmother uttered a perceptive, "Uh-hum," after she followed his gaze to a front pew where a pretty Indian girl flashed a brief smile back their way.

Spider stood, sat, and knelt at all the right times during the service, but any religious significance floated high above him along with the sweet smell of melting candle wax.

His attention focused solely on the figure in pale yellow, kneeling between her sister and stepmother. Even with her back to him, Suzy was beautiful, Spider thought. Her long silky strands were as black as the Gila Mountains against a rising sun. Such daydreaming sent him back to a simpler time on the reservation, when Grandfather Joe had taught Spider and his cousins how to survive in the desert. He wondered if those memories were what drew him to Suzy. Perhaps they were a part of his attraction to her, he thought, eager for Mass to finish. Then the twosome would linger on the sidewalk out front while Suzy's older sister, Lilly, lit candles inside and prayed.

Every Sunday, Lilly would emerge from the church, blink at the brightness, and then cast an amused glance their way. "Come on, Suzy! We have to help make dinner."

As Lilly grew large with child, Spider offered to carry her toddler son the few blocks to Suzy's house where many of the relatives gathered on Sundays. One time, Spider was asked in, and from then on, he and Suzanne Reves began seeing each other often—between classes, at lunchtime, after school, and even on weekends.

Spider's senses seemed to swim whenever Suzy came into view, and he felt a need to protect her from the jeers that spewed from the various cliques at school. But he quickly discovered his girlfriend didn't really need his help. She would set her chin slightly upturned against them, as if to mock back, "Go ahead! Call me 'squaw' or whatever you like. I am Apache and proud of it!" Spider sighed audibly when he pictured Suzy that way, a little haughty, but still shy.

At first, she didn't accept his offer of the whiskey he brought to school in his lunch sack. But after weeks of coaxing, the girl finally tried some. In spite of her tearing eyes at the strong taste, she gulped a little more just to prove she wasn't spineless.

That was the beginning of Suzy's downturn. When the couple went out with the gang on Saturday nights, she and Spider would often steal away from the rest of the group and spend long hours drinking, just the two of them in each other's arms.

Several months later, when Spider noticed his girlfriend at a remote lunch table, he knew instantly something was wrong. Suzy looked terrible. The corners of her mouth sagged, and her gloomy eyes were red and puffy from obvious crying. He could feel his heart beating anxiously as he sat down across from her and asked, "What's the matter?"

"I'm pregnant," she said bluntly.

Spider glanced around to make certain no one could eavesdrop on the conversation. "Are you sure?"

She nodded. "My sister, Lilly, said there's no doubt. And she suspects my stepmother will kick me out as soon as she discovers my … uh … condition."

Spider studied his girlfriend's face a moment before asking, "Do you think Lilly and her husband, Virgil, might adopt the baby?"

"Oh, Spider! They can hardly afford to feed their own two kids. How can they feed another one?" Her voice began to quaver. "I don't know what to do. Lilly says I won't start showing for a couple more months. I can wait until then, I suppose, to tell my stepmother."

There was a long silence between them. Spider's mind was racing ahead, imagining the humiliation Suzy would face at school when the other students found out. If they called her "squaw" now, whatever would they call her then? At that moment, he felt like smashing all their faces ahead of time. Then he suddenly came back to reality and the troubled eyes across the table.

"I'm sorry, Suzy. I never thought of this."

"Yeah, I didn't either, only of how much I care for you." She took a deep breath. "I know I've sinned, and now I have to pay for it. I haven't dared to go to confession for a long time. Oh, is the priest ever going to lecture me!"

Spider forced a grin, joking, "He'll probably give you so many *Our Fathers* and *Hail Marys* to say that you'll still be kneeling in the church when Mass starts the next morning!"

Suzy mustered a faint smile. Then her eyes began to water again. "Are you going to desert me now, Spider, like other guys do when their girls get pregnant?"

Her words stung him. "Of course, not! I love you, Suzy." He reached for her hand and squeezed it. "My love's forever," he declared.

"Thanks, Spider," she said, then stuffed a half-eaten sandwich in a bag and walked off.

Suzy seemed to take Spider's appetite along with her, because he didn't feel like touching his food. But he certainly felt the need for a long draft of whiskey to silence his clamoring thoughts. There was the shame his girlfriend faced—and the homelessness when her stepmother found out. He would be only fifteen years old when the baby came. How could a fifteen-year-old make enough money to support a girl and baby? And his father—what would Henry Montero do when he discovered his son was going to present him with a grandchild in seven months? Spider decided to hide the pregnancy from his family, too, as long as possible.

One drizzly April evening three months later, a knock at the door pulled Spider from his place in front of the television screen. Suzy stood outside, holding a stuffed cloth bag. Her hair hung in long, wet strings over her drenched clothes. Wearing only a light sweater against the weather, she shivered. "Well, it's happened. My stepmother just threw me out, and I have nowhere to go."

Spider reached his arms around her neck, and they stood there on the doorstep, hugging each other in the soft rain.

Meanwhile, his mom had wandered over to the gaping door and had sized up the situation immediately. After all, Suzy's rain-soaked dress clung to her, emphasizing the bulge at her waistline.

Mrs. Montero seized the girl's hand. "Come and get yourself dried off and into some other clothes! Then we'll talk," she said. The children sitting around stared in silence.

Privacy was nonexistent in such small quarters. But for some semblance of it, the mother ordered all the children to bed—including Mary Ann—before turning her attention to Suzy's and Spider's problem.

First, she spoke directly to her son, "If you're old enough to make babies, then you're old enough to make money. Get yourself a job—tomorrow!"

Spider soberly nodded, then shrugged toward Suzy. "What about her?"

"She'll stay here, of course!"

"But what will … will …?"

A hint of a smile played at his mother's mouth. "We just won't tell your father for now. He has too much on his mind. Whenever he's here, Suzy will stay upstairs in the little storage space. At other times, she can go where she pleases in the house." Then his mother added sternly, "And both of you will stay in school."

Spider grimaced at her words. Many of the students had already guessed Suzy's condition and were making her life miserable. And how was he supposed to work plus attend school? Suddenly, he realized summer vacation would begin in about six weeks. Then Suzy could rest from all the taunts, stay sheltered in his family's home, and wait until the baby came in late August.

During the months that followed, Henry Montero rose with his usual hangover every morning at 5:30 a.m., dressed, and then stumbled out the door to work at the laundry. Late every night, he would stumble back in, collapse on the sofa, and promptly pass out—never realizing that a fourteen-year-old Indian girl was crouching in the attic space overhead, waiting to slip down the ladder to rejoin the family.

Spider became a very busy person during those months, selling daily newspapers—and marijuana for a neighborhood dealer. He saved his money carefully, waiting for the birth of the baby.

About a month before Suzy's delivery date, Henry Montero disappeared again. "Maybe he's gone back to the reservation," his wife told her eldest son. "I know of many places there where your father can live easily off the land and streams, never worrying about making money and feeding so many mouths."

Spider felt distressed. Now he was responsible for not only Suzy and the expected newborn, but also for helping to feed and care for his mother and siblings. Although he realized his grandmother and a few other relatives would share that responsibility, he knew the need for finances was great. Therefore, he stepped up his marijuana business, adding other drugs to his sales list.

When September arrived, Grandmother delivered her newest great-grandchild, Anthony.

"Oh! He's beautiful!" Lilly crooned over the box that served as cradle. Suzy's older sister went on about his looks and then turned to the girl. "I'll help you care for him, so you can go back to school when it starts."

Suzy nodded, smiling. "Yes, I need to stay in school if I can."

Although all the windows stood open, the little garage-house seemed to steam in the summer heat, making the baby fuss. Suzy picked him up and walked Lilly to the door, saying good-bye.

Turning back, she exclaimed, "Look at him, Spider! He *is* beautiful."

Spider raised his eyebrows, teasing, "Of course! The kid looks just like me." Then he quickly turned sober. "Is he worth it, Suzy?"

She understood. Was little Anthony worth all the ridicule she had endured over the past half year? Spider watched her survey the small round face, the black curls framing it, and the large dark eyes that gazed around wonderingly. "I would go through it all again and again to have such a sweet child," she said.

Cuddling the baby, Suzy added, "It would have been much better to have done it right—you know, get married first, then start having babies. But I can't undo what is done. And look what we have!"

Out of the blue, Spider announced, "I've found a place for you and Anthony."

"A place?"

"Yes, it's a tiny house a few blocks over. I've rented it for you. And even after school starts, I'll keep up my businesses, so you'll always have rent and food."

"That'll be nice." She looked around at the small home. "Your mother was so kind to take me in, but it's been very crowded here—and now especially, with the baby, too!"

"You're family, Suzy."

The girl gazed down at her child again. "You know, Spider, my mother died when I was six, and no one seemed to want me—except Lilly. But she wasn't much older than I was. I've never had much, and anything I've managed to get has been taken away. Now I have something that's all mine. And he's perfect." Her words had dropped to a whisper, but Spider could hear the pride in her voice.

After Suzy and little Anthony moved into the rental, Spider visited every evening to play with the baby or to help with housework. Sometimes, the young father even bathed the child. Anthony was growing fast, and with each week, he seemed to grow even more handsome, like a little dark cherub with dimpled cheeks—so cuddly and playful.

After Suzy had returned to school, Lilly, Spider's grandmother, and Mrs. Montero took turns caring for Anthony. Henry Montero returned from his out-of-state venture and readily accepted his new grandson. At first, he had grumbled somewhat, but the baby won his affection in no time. In fact, with all the uncles, aunts, and other relatives, little Anthony received more than a child's share of attention and love.

Then one spring morning, when the baby was six months old, he awoke with a croupy cough. Stopping by on his way to school, Spider suggested Suzy stay home and call Lilly. "See if she can take you to the doctor today. The kid don't look too good."

"I will," she promised.

That afternoon, when the young father discovered Anthony had been hospitalized for pneumonia, Spider's first impulse was to rush to the hospital. But his mother persuaded him to stay.

"Go sell your papers first!" she ordered. "You'll really need that money now."

Spider obeyed, cringing. *If my mother only knew what else I'm selling!*

Later, he borrowed his cousin's motorcycle and made his way to the medical center, where his baby looked terribly small in a large hospital crib. "What did the doctor say?" he asked his girlfriend.

"He thinks Anthony'll get well all right," Suzy replied. "But he has to stay here a long time—maybe two weeks."

Then they both heard Lilly's voice at the doorway. "Ah! Poor little Anthony!" she cooed quietly, not wanting to wake him. She winced at the needle feeding into his frail leg. "I feel like he's part mine, you know."

Suzy tried to smile, but she looked as if the effort alone might exhaust her. She also had noticed new bruises on her sister's arm and face. For some time, Suzy had suspected Lilly's husband Virgil of abuse, but the older sister always denied it and made excuses for her injuries.

"Do you want me to stay with Anthony tonight?" Lilly offered. "Virgil still hasn't found a job, so he could watch our two."

"No, thank you!" Suzy said. "I don't want to leave my baby."

By the next morning, Lilly was dead, shot by her own husband.

Remaining at the hospital by Anthony's crib, Suzy bore her grief stoically. Then the day of the funeral she left the baby long enough to attend the service at the barrio church.

Spider stood protectively at her side and worried at the tears she held back. "It wouldn't hurt you to go ahead and cry," he whispered. "Look! Even your stepmother is bawling."

Suzy ignored him and stood as stonily as she had stood months before against the onslaughts of schoolmates.

After his two-week stay in the hospital, Baby Anthony returned to his own cradle box, while Spider and Suzy watched him together that first evening home. After he was asleep, the couple made sandwiches in the kitchen, smoked a few more cigarettes, and talked. Spider was trying to get his girlfriend to open up about Lilly and her tragic death.

All of a sudden, Suzy gasped. "Something's wrong!" She raced to the box that held her son. "He's not breathing!" she screamed.

Spider bounded over to the baby and picked him up, shaking him gently. "Breathe, boy, breathe!" The small round face was unresponsive, the lips blue. "Call an ambulance—quick!" he hollered, then tried pushing on the baby's ribs to get them to move. Nothing.

Fighting off the horror that engulfed him, Spider begged, *Oh, God! Please, don't let him die!*

CHAPTER 6

AFTER THE CHIVAROS

Baby Anthony died, and for days, Suzanne Reves sat in a stupor. Spider tried to coax her from the lethargy, but she neither smiled nor cried. She just stared wordlessly, sheltering any thoughts behind her thick eyelashes.

Caring for the girl, Grandmother reminded Spider, "We are family. We are all Apache." The elderly woman had washed the long silken hair and was now brushing it as it tumbled over the slender shoulders. Even when a comb found knots in the black strands, Suzy remained still and unflinching.

Spider fought an urge to shake the girl, to rouse her from the dream world she had sunk into. "Will she ever come out of this?" he asked.

The plump woman shook her head. "I don't know. She's had too much sadness in her life. First, her mamma dies.

Then her new mama don't want her. A child knows. A child hurts when no love is there. Then Lilly, the sister who helped raise her, she is shot and killed. And now, little Anthony is gone. That's too much—too, too much for one girl. Her mind has built a strong wall against the hurt. And that hurt is deep inside, a hurt in her spirit. I don't know if that wall will come down."

Spider's own heart felt raw and swollen. He, too, had seen death snatch away loved ones: Magdalena, Grandfather Joe, and his own baby son. Now Suzy was acting as if she were dead. She breathed; she even ate if Grandmother fed her. But her large, dark eyes stared past them both into some soft, safe world.

Spider dealt with his heartache in the only way he knew. He bought and drank more liquor. Taking a fresh pint to school with him every morning, he usually had it drained when the last bell rang each afternoon.

One of his gang members noticed and expressed concern. "Hey! What d'ya tryin' to do, Chico?" Marbles kidded him. "Drink yerself into an early grave?"

Grave wasn't a good word to use. It only drove Spider's mind to the unmarked, newly turned earth that held a small body. Defiantly, Spider reached back into the locker, retrieved the bottle, and in full view, tilted it to his lips.

"What is this?" A deep voice startled him, a voice belonging to Mr. Lucas, the vice-principal.

Everything whirled in that moment—a picture of Suzy's vacant stare, Baby Anthony turning blue in his arms—and an anger boiled up from his stomach that filled Spider with such rage he turned on the man. "What's it to ya?" he growled.

"Give me that!" Mr. Lucas grabbed at the bottle, and Spider winced as glass shattered against the wall, draining its precious liquid at his feet.

He screamed at the man, "Now, look what you've done!" then clenched the remaining jagged glass like a knife, prodding the air with it threateningly.

Mr. Lucas leaped backward, shouting, "You're through here! Leave the books and clean the junk from your locker! You're expelled."

Spider's hand went limp, and he suddenly felt sick to his stomach. The hallway had grown quiet, and he noticed a blur of faces, including that of Marbles, all gaping at him.

Scooping his few belongings out of the locker, Spider pushed his way through the students. He slowed to a deliberate, casual stroll as he left school for the last time.

Outside, he felt for change in his jeans pocket. There was enough for bus fare to his cousin's place. Spider's cousin rode with a motorcycle gang and now had taken the name, "Crazy Ray." Ray would have plenty of beer on hand to soothe the boy's raw nerves. Spider couldn't go home just then. He couldn't bear to face his mother and grandmother, who had preached to him repeatedly about the value of an education in getting a good job. He couldn't bear his mother's well-worn speech, "You don't want to pick vegetables all your life." And most of all, Spider couldn't face the empty stare on Suzanne's beautiful face—not now.

For several days, he stayed at his cousin's, where the beer flowed freely, and he helped monkey-wrench on a motorcycle, a "panhead" with only a few quirks to work out.

"If you can learn how to keep this thing humming," Ray said, "maybe I'll just give it to ya for your birthday."

When summer came, Ray kept his promise and presented Spider with the cycle, opening whole new vistas to the sixteen-year-old. No longer was Spider trapped in the grimy streets of Watts. Now he could ride wherever he pleased, even rocket along back roads to the east where fertile fields and fresh air revived his spirits.

A few weeks after Anthony's death, Suzy's stepmother had taken the girl back into her house. Although Suzy's mental state was improving, she remained in a depression that leeched out any enthusiasm for life. To complicate the situation, the girl took up drinking with the same passion that Spider had.

The closest Suzy came to her former self was when she was perched behind Spider on the cycle, flying along backcountry roads. "Hit it!" she would cry in his ear. And he would respond with more throttle, lurching forward, making Suzy squeal while her hair streamed behind them like a long, black banner.

By then, Spider had graduated from his school gang, the Chivaros, to an older, more experienced gang. His sixteenth year was filled with activities involving these new friends, whose lives centered on motorcycles, drinking, and drugs.

Dropping the newspaper sales altogether, Spider expanded his illegal business to a wider area. With wheels now, he could make much more money peddling various drugs.

To toughen his image, Spider bought leather to wear and added tattoos to his arms and chest. He rarely returned to his parents' house anymore. His appearance only brought his mother grief. After all, her child, the boy who had run alongside her father not many years before, had turned into a hardened alcoholic, a leather-jacketed motorcycle gang member. But Spider hadn't hardened enough to become insensitive to her feelings. Therefore, he spared those feelings by staying away as much as possible.

One thing he couldn't avoid, though, was the constant gnawing fear of getting caught with the drugs he peddled. "If that happens, who would take care of Suzy?" he fretted. He felt he was the only one left who genuinely cared for the girl. In her chronic state of depression, Suzy was incapable of caring for herself. And Spider became obsessed with moneymaking, so he could buy his girlfriend beautiful clothes and shoes, the fancy things she had never owned before.

Just days after Spider's seventeenth birthday, he was cruising the dark, tinseled streets of downtown Los Angeles. Lagging at the end of the cycles' pack, he picked his way through the nighttime clutter of pedestrians and traffic.

Spotting some open space ahead, he gunned the motor and charged straight through an unseen red light. A yell and a strangely muted *thump* brought Spider to a crashing standstill.

A cracked headlight revealed the twisted body of a bearded man sprawled by the cycle. The man was obviously a vagrant, one of the many winos who roamed that section of the city.

In his own inebriated state, Spider's heart hammered against his chest while the image of his sister under a truck tire flashed on and off in his mixed-up mind.

A crowd was gathering, closing in on him while he gazed nervously around. On impulse, he hopped back aboard his cycle and tried the motor. When it sprang to life, he raced off amid yells and curses.

A half-hour later, Spider Montero stood in his parents' house, hastily stuffing clothes into a saddlebag. His mother stood numbly by, begging, "Please, son, you'll have to run forever. When they catch you, it'll be much worse. Phone the police now before …"

Her words were cut off by the sound of pounding at the front door. Reluctantly, she opened it to several policemen.

Realizing the futility of trying to escape, Spider squarely faced the uniforms and heard the dreaded words, "The man you hit is dead. You're under arrest."

Chapter 7

DRINK DEMONS

Spider gripped the bars, trying to steady his hands. He had been locked in jail—and without a drink—for nearly two days. With the first pangs of alcohol withdrawal threatening, he felt restless, pacing back and forth in the small cell.

"I need a drink," he muttered. The judge had set bail too high for family or friends to free him. And, instead of remorse for the vagrant tagged "John Doe" lying on a slab in the morgue, Spider felt only thirst, an overwhelming thirst for anything laced with alcohol.

In the close, hot air, his jail uniform seemed glued to his sweaty skin. As the hours rolled on, he perspired even more and began to shake violently. Throwing himself on a cot, he tried to calm down, but his body wouldn't obey.

At last, in desperation, he cried out, "I need a drink—please! Just one drink!" Bawdy laughter and remarks shot back from other cells.

"Don't we all, half-breed!"

"Yeah, man! We all'd like to party!"

"Hey, guard! How 'bout a round of drinks?"

As his head hammered painfully, Spider's eyes couldn't focus anymore. Then, when the lights dimmed for the night, shadows took on strange, monstrous forms like hairy-legged creatures clinging to and crawling all over the cell. Spider slapped his hands across his eyes, but he could still see them. They were attacking in one large mass.

"Ayeee!" he screamed in terror. "Get 'em away!" Vainly, he boxed at the hallucinations in the air.

"Quiet down, man!"—"How can a fella sleep anyhow?" came the complaints around him.

But Spider was deaf to them all. Deep in the throes of the DTs (delirium tremens), he honestly believed himself caught in a giant web while monstrous, hairy-legged creatures closed in on him.

He screamed and screamed until guards carried him off to a different cell where he couldn't hurt himself or disturb other inmates. But the hallucinations followed, chasing the seventeen-year-old around in circles until he fell in a heap on the padded floor.

Helplessly, his eyes rolled toward the ceiling where hundreds more of the hairy tarantulas appeared to be descending upon him. Again, he screamed. He wept. He vomited. He shook violently, which made his entire body ache like one huge muscle spasm.

During a few fleeting rational moments, Spider became even more terrified. What was happening to him? Had he lost his mind completely? Recalling his grandmother's description of alcoholism as the "drink demon," he sneered. This wasn't one demon, he thought. They were many, and they were trying to snuff out his life.

"No!" he shouted. "I can't die." Who would take care of Suzy? He had to stay alive, and he had to get out of jail. He had to make money for beautiful Suzanne Reves. He forced himself to think only of her: of her straight, white teeth behind a broad smile—the way she used to smile before Lilly and Baby Anthony had died.

The imaginings turned again into hallucinations, this time slithering snakes. He gasped for breath, his heart beating wildly, until he sank once more to the floor, exhausted.

Suddenly, a voice called to him, "Hey, man! You look bad."

Spider tried to focus on the bearded face peering through the tiny barred hole in the door, but the image blurred. He knew the voice, however. It belonged to one of his gang brothers.

The voice had dropped to a whisper. "I got some friends in here, and that's how come I got to see ya. I brought ya some—uh—medicine, Spider." A small plastic bag poked through the bars. "This'll fix ya up fast. Sorry, I couldn't get here sooner!"

Spider pulled himself up, groped for the bag and, fumbling, popped a capsule into his mouth. Managing a weak *"Gracias!"* he sank back onto the floor.

The whisper warned, "Keep that stuff hid, man, or we're both in trouble!" Then the visitor added, "And, Chico, as soon as you're well, try to get work in the kitchen. I hear some of the guys in there stir up a mean brew."

Not too long after the gang member left, Spider fell into a deep sleep, his first real rest in three days. When he awoke, big burley hands were pulling him to his feet.

The guard offered him some soap. "Wash off all the puke, boy, 'cause ya gotta earn your keep now that you're doin' better."

Spider was able to follow his buddy's advice and get a job in the kitchen. There, he found the coveted "brew" that kept the DTs at a safe distance. "I never want to go through that again," he breathed. "Never!"

Meanwhile, his mother, grandmother, and Suzy visited him every Sunday afternoon. And sometimes his cousin, Crazy Ray, would drop by, or one of the other gang members would smuggle in another bag of "medicine."

Except for Sunday visitation, time held no meaning for Spider. One hour drifting into another formed his tedious day-to-day existence. He rose, he ate, and he methodically washed dishes, day after boring day.

Suzy always dressed her best when she visited him, and she put on a brave face. But, oftentimes, tears would betray her, and she would break down. "I can't stand the thought of you going to prison for years," she told him. "You're my only love."

Spider's fist paled as he pressed it against the glass that separated them. He, too, dreaded the thought of prison. It was rumored that authorities were stricter there, and booze and drugs were harder to come by. Also, he had heard horror stories of life in the state penitentiary, where even the toughest of gang members became putty in the hands of hardened convicts.

Every time Suzy left the visitor's cubicle, sadness would settle like a chill upon Spider. Then he would take comfort from the contents of the hidden bag or from the special "brew" in the jail's kitchen.

After several months of waiting for trial, Spider was led at last into a courtroom and seated at a table. He felt like a spectator at someone else's hearing, not his own. He heard a public defender, with whom he had talked only a few times, say something about "first offense." Then other unfamiliar legal jargon bombarded him.

Finally, Spider stood before the grim-faced judge who gave him a choice, "Fifteen years in prison or enlist in the army!"

"He'll enlist, Your Honor," snapped the public defender, and Spider nodded in agreement.

An hour later, after checking out of the jail, Spider was met by his grinning cousin. "Woo-hoo!" Crazy Ray shouted as he led the way to a Harley Davidson parked outside. "That was close. You nearly got sent up!"

Dizzy with his sudden freedom, Spider agreed. Then he asked, "Ray, have you got anything to drink?"

"Of course!" the man roared. "You can go pick up Suzy later, and we'll all celebrate your freedom." He let out another whoop as they jumped aboard the cycle and sped off.

The following week, Spider Montero locked hands with Suzanne Reves as they stood before a priest inside Los Angeles' historic mission church. A vision in light blue, Suzy softly repeated her marriage vows. Then the groom did the same, while family members and a few friends witnessed the simple ceremony.

After only a weekend together as husband and wife, Spider left Suzy in the care of some friends while he went off to basic training. "Don't worry, Mrs. Montero!" he teased his bride. "I'm not leaving you already. As soon as boot camp's over, I'll carry you off to wherever I'm stationed."

Spider kept his word, taking his bride with him to an army base in Colorado. He was charged with new hope that the change in location would bring Suzy out of her depressed mental state. But after a few months, Spider realized her condition remained unchanged. She slept in late and lounged around their apartment the rest of the day, trying to drink away her depression and boredom.

Spider's alcoholism, too, followed him to Colorado. But he didn't allow it to interfere with his job on the base. He kept up a respectable front. After all, he lectured himself, if he wasn't successful with this stint in the army, the judge would send him off to prison. And besides, the beautiful, mountainous state of Colorado was a welcome alternative to prison bars.

Spider tried to get his wife interested in local events. He took her to rodeos and the base theater. Sometimes her eyes would flicker with pleasure momentarily as she seemed to emerge from her sad world. But those times were brief and rare.

One evening, she met him with the words, "I think I'm pregnant," then burst out sobbing, "I can't! I can't!"

Spider spread his arms around her. "You can't what?"

"I can't lose another baby, like we did Anthony. No! I'd rather die." She was inconsolable for hours.

The next day Spider visited a base doctor, who suggested the young private bring in his wife. After her office visit, the doctor called Spider at work.

"Your wife is in a deep state of depression," he said. "I have strong doubts about her ability to care properly for the baby when it arrives. Even with treatment, I don't think she'd be well enough for that kind of responsibility."

The doctor hesitated before asking, "Does your wife drink, Private Montero?"

"Some," Spider lied.

"Well, that complicates matters. If you have any dependable relatives who'd be willing to take the baby—at least for a while—I'd advise that. Or you could put it up for adoption."

Spider mumbled his thanks, then began to brood. How could he give up his own flesh and blood for adoption? And what about his and Suzy's Indian heritage? He didn't want his child to miss out on that rich culture. At the same time, he didn't want his child to grow up in the seething streets of Watts, either. Unemployment, low wages, and racial tensions, combined with rampant drug use, were festering in his former neighborhood. He expected it to explode someday soon like a giant raging volcano. No, he didn't want any child of his growing up in Watts.

Then a thought struck him—*the reservation!* Maybe some relatives of his or Suzy's on the San Carlos Indian Reservation would want to raise the child. His family had, indeed, been poor in Arizona, but his brightest memories focused on things money couldn't buy: the rapport between him and his grandfather, their rich Indian culture, the hunting and fishing, the wild openness of the place, the sunsets, even the comforting sound of coyotes singing him to sleep at night.

After discussing the situation with Suzy, Spider began writing letters, beginning with his own mother. She replied with several possibilities and included addresses.

When Suzy's delivery time drew close, Spider placed a phone call to San Carlos, Arizona. By the time the baby girl arrived, a beaming Indian couple was there to spirit her away.

Spider accompanied them to the parking lot. "I hope you don't mind, but I checked with the council and other people who know you well. They all said you're good people."

The bronze-faced woman flashed him a warm smile as she cuddled the baby closer. "Don't worry, Spider! We will give your little one lots of love. And she'll be baptized at the mission as soon as we get back home."

"That's good," Spider said with a catch in his throat. He found himself wishing he could undo the lives he and Suzanne had lived thus far. He truly wanted to be a father to his little girl.

When they reached the car, he awkwardly pulled back the receiving blanket and gazed down at his sleeping daughter. Her hair, as dark and curly as his own, clung to her well-shaped head. "She reminds me a lot of my younger sister, Magdalena, the one who died." Feeling the sting of tears, Spider quickly turned away. "Take good care of her!" he called over his shoulder and then shuffled back across the parking lot.

CHAPTER 8

BULLETS AND BLAZES

The remaining two years in Colorado seemed to help Suzanne climb out of the pit where she had languished for so long. She began socializing with other military wives—and even attended Mass at the base chapel on the Sunday mornings she wasn't too "hung over." Spider avoided the chapel altogether.

When his army tenure ended, the Monteros drove their recently purchased 1949 Chevy back to Watts. Almost immediately, Spider found a job at a candy factory.

Suzy was pregnant again, but this time her eyes glistened in eager anticipation for the baby, which was due in January. Every payday, Spider revealed his own excitement when he bought toys or tiny T-shirts and booties for the expected newcomer.

Considering himself a true family man now, Spider determined to provide for his wife and child. In Watts only a few days, however, he sensed a new unrest in his old neighborhood. This prompted him to seek a way out even sooner than planned. Life in the well-regulated army had changed his way of viewing the world. Watts suddenly looked shabbier than his memories of the place. And the faces of his Chicano neighbors seemed drained of all hope. Moreover, there was a new defiance in the air. His black neighbors, especially, were tired of watching well-to-do, white Californians rise to higher levels of prosperity, with their fancy homes and cars, while minorities seemed trapped in low-wage jobs—and the same cramped area of south-central Los Angeles.

Although the latest federal civil rights legislation was plodding through Congress, the bigotry locked in many people's minds stubbornly refused to budge. In California, the 1963 Rumford Act, which had forbidden racial discrimination in the sale or rental of residential property, was now under siege by Proposition 14 in the upcoming November election. That proposition sought to undo the antidiscrimination laws long battled for in the western state. It threatened to keep minority Californians caged in their slums. They weren't the high-rise slums of the East with their narrow streets, but they were slums just the same: rented houses—not owned— overcrowded and in dismal repair.

Although Spider knew little about politics and Proposition 14, he still sensed the growing unease around him. Therefore, he and Suzy escaped as often as possible to San Bernardino Valley where her brothers lived. While visiting there, Spider began filling out job applications.

"We've got to get out of Watts soon," he warned his wife one day after work. "This place feels like a warehouse stuffed with dynamite, just waiting to go off."

"What do you mean?" she asked, her arms resting gently on her rounded stomach.

"People at the factory are boiling mad," he told her. "Some law got voted in that, they say, means whites can keep blacks and other people of color out of their uppity neighborhoods." Spider shook his head. "I'm telling you, Suzy, this whole thing could turn into another Civil War. People are ready to fight. And before they do, I've got to get you out of here."

The next day, as Spider was leaving the house for work, he noticed some suspicious-looking teenagers loitering near his Chevy. "Hey!" he called out. "Get away ..."

Before he could finish, shots rang out as pain seared through his leg, and he crumpled to the ground. Spider barely heard Suzy's terrified scream before he blacked out. Awakening later in an ambulance, he grasped the attendant's arm. "My wife?" he pleaded.

"She's fine. In fact, she's following behind us in your car. You take it easy, *amigo*! You've lost a lot of blood."

In the hospital, Spider mended quickly. He soon returned home, more determined than ever to get out of Watts. As if in answer to his desperation, Spider found a job soon thereafter with a trash collection firm in San Bernardino. He also found a house there just in time for the arrival of little Lydia on January 21, 1964.

Watching Suzy tenderly nurse the newborn left no doubt in Spider's mind that his wife would now make a good mother. She seemed truly contented for the first time since Baby Anthony's death. And during those early days in Lydia's life, a new, easy intimacy sprang up between the husband and wife as they shared in caring for the baby. That intimacy was short-lived, but it bloomed anyway, however brief the promise of what could be.

Every weekday, Spider would rise at 3:00 a.m. and drive his garbage truck from four o'clock to ten-thirty in the morning. Sometime around noon, he would return home and pry open a bottle of beer. His cousin, Crazy Ray, and other gang buddies began dropping by some afternoons, and they would all party together at the Montero house.

At that time, Spider didn't recognize any similarity between his father's drinking habits and his own. "After all," he rationalized, "I'm home with the wife and kid—not off at some bar away from my family." Seemingly untouched by the noise and confusion around her, Baby Lydia slept peacefully through it all.

The Monteros had escaped Watts none too soon. On the evening of August 11, 1965, when Lydia was eighteen months old, Spider's former neighborhood did, indeed, erupt in war. After an unbearable, sweltering day, a highway patrolman had tried to arrest a black man for drunk driving. The incident swelled into a riot and finally into all-out warfare, with looting, burning, and gunfire.

When news of the riots found Spider, he was about to retire for the night. Studying his wife's swollen form already settled in bed, Spider began to play tug-of-war with his emotions. Suzy was expecting another baby who could come early, the doctor had warned. But Spider felt compelled to arm himself and head at once to his parents' place to help protect them and their property. At the same time, he didn't dare leave Suzy and Lydia unguarded. And he certainly didn't want to jeopardize their lives by taking them into the war zone.

Suzy opened her eyes and smiled lazily. "What's wrong?"

When Spider explained his quandary, she insisted upon going along with him. "We must protect your grandmother and the rest of the family. It's part of our tradition, you know."

"But, Suzy," he protested, "this is why I got us out of Watts in the first place, so you wouldn't be there when this happened! It'd be foolish to take you back just when everything's falling apart."

His wife had already gotten up and was dressing. "It would be foolish to leave me here when your grandmother's a midwife. She could deliver the baby if it comes early. And, anyway," she said smugly, "I can handle a gun just as well as you can."

Suzy was stuffing clean diapers, bottles, and canned milk into bags. She pointed to her suitcase, which she had already packed for the hospital. "Could you take that out to the car? I'll get Lydia."

Spider didn't argue, but he did order his wife to sit in the back seat with the baby. "It'll be safer," he declared.

Long before they neared Watts, the couple could see the glow of runaway fires lighting the night sky. Spider's heart raced anxiously. Would he get there in time to help his family? Or was it already too late?

The next hour became the longest of Spider's life as he drove like a crazed man, dodging the melee around him. He felt caught in a maze, the smoke hanging like a thick smothering blanket overhead. Each time he got within a few blocks of his parents' place, a roadblock or mob would force him to retreat and take a different route.

It had finally happened. His section of the city was writhing in agony. The years of pent-up frustration were visible everywhere like angry, oozing sores.

"Keep your heads down!" Spider shouted when he heard bullets ricochet nearby.

A giggle sounded from the back seat. "No need to worry, *mi esposo*! We're as flat on the floor as we can get."

At long last, Spider guided the Chevy the final few feet toward his grandmother's front yard. Scurrying to the door, he pounded on it. "It's Spider. Let us in!" he hollered.

His youngest brother, Jesse, opened the door while his mother tugged at the six-year-old. "Go back to bed and stay down!" Her voice sounded strained. Sirens were screaming everywhere, and gunshots popped in the distance like harmless fireworks on the Fourth of July.

Quickly, Spider hustled Suzy, Lydia, and the various bags through the yard and into the house.

"Your father's holding down our place," his mother said, "while the kids and I stay here with Grandma."

Spider cast an amused glance at the old woman sleeping blissfully on the couch. Nearby, a lone candle flickered. "Are all the windows and doors locked?" he asked.

Mrs. Montero nodded, gazing around at the blinds that shrouded the living room windows. She sighed loudly. "I'm glad you came, son. I feel so helpless—and scared."

Her words boosted Spider's courage as he gathered boxes of ammunition and found a post to keep watch near the front window. "Get some sleep, Mom! There's no telling how long this will last."

It lasted six days. And after the police and military were able to restore some semblance of order to Watts, thirty-four persons were dead, and over one thousand people had suffered from wounds inflicted during the riots. Property damage was estimated at $40 million.

Grandmother's house and the smaller Montero place came through the ordeal unscathed. But some of their neighbors weren't as fortunate. While Spider walked through the smoldering remains of the local business section, a sickening sadness followed him. *This is stupid! People wiping out what little they have.* With many of the businesses destroyed, he realized, the neighborhood would become even poorer than before. Gone were the jobs those businesses had supplied the community.

Suzy looked upset when Spider returned to help pack up the car for their trip home. As soon as they were underway, her words came rushing, "Your grandmother said I was carrying a *boy*." Then she covered her face and cried, "I can't bear to lose another son, like our Anthony."

Spider was surprised by the outburst. "But, Suzy, look at Lydia, how healthy she is! You're being silly. Just because we lost Anthony doesn't mean we'll lose other sons." He pulled the car to the side of the street and enclosed her with his arms. "You've come so far, *mi amor*. You've been so brave this past week—so strong. Be brave with this next baby too," he challenged. "I know he'll make you even happier. Just wait and see!"

His grandmother had predicted correctly. The child, born October 20, 1965, was a boy—Robert—and Suzy genuinely loved him, becoming quite busy with an infant plus a toddler to care for.

Meanwhile, Spider's gang *compadres* continued to use the Montero home as a gathering place. Sometimes twenty motorcycles were parked outside while beer and other drinks flowed lavishly inside. Just as Lydia had learned to sleep through the commotion, so did Baby Robert.

Spider had repaired a 1958 Harley-Davidson and had begun riding on "TNT" (tavern to tavern) runs with his friends. Because another child meant more expenses, the young father began once more to supplement his income from the straight job by selling drugs on the side. Suzy objected, and that difference of opinion lit the fuse for many a fight.

"You're gonna get caught and land in jail again!" she yelled one night after the couple and several other gang members had gotten quite drunk. Fixing her bleary eyes upon her husband, Suzy yelled even louder, "And when they slap you in prison, who's gonna keep Lydia and Robert and me in food and rent? Just tell me that!"

Spider's retort slurred as he shouted back, "It's because of you and the kids that I'm selling! My job don't make enough." In that moment he nearly confessed his constant fear while peddling drugs—the fear of being caught and arrested—also the ever-present specter of competing gangs lurking on the shadowy fringes like wild animals ready to pounce and tear him to pieces. But his *machismo* kept him from admitting those fears in front of his friends.

Suzy grabbed his keys and took off on the Harley, leaving her husband to brood and to drink even more. The combination of hurt, guilt, and worry churned with the alcohol and sent Spider's spirits plummeting until he grumbled, "I'm better off dead." Withdrawing a .45 revolver from the cupboard, Spider put the barrel to his skull. Just as he pulled the trigger, a hand slapped at the gun and sent the bullet careening through the kitchen wall. This time the noise did wake the children.

The friend who saved Spider's life had sobered instantly. He emptied the gun of its bullets and put his host to bed, guarding him until Suzy returned home.

In March, a chill hung in the air the afternoon Spider hopped onto his cycle and headed south where some of his cousins lived. As he rode, he enjoyed the scenery: the valley and hills sparkling after a recent rain while the sun dropped ever closer to the sea.

With his trench coat flapping out on both sides, he resembled a large black bat—on wheels. Bending into the wind, Spider mulled over the reasons for the trip. He needed to increase his sales territory, increase the number of regular customers by branching out into his cousins' small city. Prospects were good there, he had heard.

Parking his cycle a few blocks from a relative's place, Spider began his scouting expedition on foot. With dusk, the downtown area was coming to life as theater marquees lit up and tavern lights glared out over wet sidewalks.

Taking a shortcut, Spider froze halfway through an alley. What he saw filled him with ice-cold fear as an old Apache warning replayed in his mind: *Don't go into it. There might be a mountain lion in there, waiting to attack you.* But these weren't mountain lions emerging from the shadows around him. They were eight scowling young men. And instead of savage teeth, switchblades glistened in the dim light.

"Who's this stepping through our turf?" mocked one scar-faced youth.

"Looks like Little Brown Riding Hood!" sang out another.

A tingling shiver turned Spider's forearms to gooseflesh, but he kept his anxiety well hidden behind a smirk. With the gap between his opponents closing fast, every muscle in Spider's body grew taut as his mind clicked rapidly, searching for their weakest point.

The instant he found it, he darted between two of the slowest hoodlums, catching them off guard and shoving one aside. Narrowly escaping the clutches of the other, he sprinted back up the alley. Spider felt his trench coat being ripped from his body, then a sharp blade slashed down his back. Still, he raced on through the inky darkness toward the lights ahead and the safety of the sidewalk.

Unaware if his pursuers had given up their chase, Spider kept running until he reached his cycle and sped off. He traveled the entire distance back to San Bernardino without realizing blood was oozing from the long gash in his back. Spider wouldn't have cared about the wound anyway. In those moments, he was riding high, giddy with the sense of survival.

Later, while Suzy doctored the wound, she preached to him, "You're gonna get killed for sure, Spider Montero, and leave me alone with these two kids—orphans!"

Too weakened from the loss of blood, for once Spider let his wife ramble on without interruption. Soon she ran out of ire, and her voice softened. "Oh, Spider! Please don't get yourself killed. *Te quiero, mi esposo.*" Her touch turned tender as he drifted off to sleep.

Ignoring his wife's fears, Spider continued the illegal dealing and riding with the motorcycle gang. One night, a new stock of "supplies" filled his cycle's saddlebags as he rode out of town. Spider would soon discover that others apparently knew about the valuable cargo on board.

Except for a patch of moonlight ahead, the countryside was shrouded in darkness as his cycle sped along a lonely road that headed for the Nevada border. After a while, Spider became aware of an engine throbbing far behind. As it neared, its headlights locked on him, and with the keen sense of one hunted, Spider immediately realized the danger and gunned his Harley—but not in time.

The truck bumped the bike and sent it and the rider flying to the side of the road. Gravel chewed into Spider's face as his body skidded to a stop. Spitting dirt from his mouth, he tried to stand, but the thugs fell upon him in a flash. A blow to his head sent Spider plummeting over an embankment. His attackers scrambled after him, driving their iron fists into his stomach and ribs. Spider tried to defend himself, but the head wound had left him powerless. Again and again they beat him, sending his mind back, back to that terror-filled night on the reservation. He felt just as helpless in that moment as he had as a five-year-old child.

Spider tumbled over and over, coming to a rest in a ravine. Leaving him to die, the culprits climbed back up to the Harley, which was hidden in a tangle of brush. Stripping off its saddlebags, they fled.

Spider knew no one would see him down in that hole. Even his motorcycle was hidden. Realizing he was bleeding internally, he could feel himself already slipping into shock. His mind spun wildly, weaving vivid memories. Grandfather Joe's soft, patient voice ... The hot sun sinking behind the mountains, cooling the desert ... Father Morton's warm smile ... Chubby little Magdalena hugging him fiercely ... Suzanne Reves recognizing him the first time at school ... Then, more recently, her voice scolding, "You're gonna get killed for sure, Spider Montero, and leave me alone with these two kids ..."

"I'm sorry, Suzy," he whispered as unconsciousness overtook him.

CHAPTER 9

GANGS, GOD, AND A GOOD SAMARITAN

Spider felt himself struggling, climbing upward out of a desolate and dark pit. But, strangely, not a muscle in his body moved. A remote female voice floated somewhere ahead of him, calling, "Dr. Hamilton, please report to surgery. Dr. Hamilton ..."

Spider continued his struggle, this time against the locks on his eyelids. He concentrated, opening them slowly, first to a bright white blur and then focusing on some tubes that linked his arm to a bottle overhead and an odd, square contraption beside him.

Hearing a muffled cough nearby, Spider turned toward a blue uniform belonging to a policeman, who leveled a steely gaze upon him. "So, you've finally come around!" he said. Spider licked his dry lips with an equally dry tongue and tried to respond, but only a gravelly sound came out. The man leaned forward, informing Spider in a stern voice, "I don't really like you and what you stand for, but there's someone in the hall you need to thank."

Puzzled, Spider watched the officer move to the doorway, where a stocky, middle-aged man bounded into the room, a wide grin crinkling his sunburned face. "You're awake—finally!" he exclaimed.

The man lowered his large frame onto a chair beside the bed and began to relate an incredible story. "I was driving to Nevada yesterday evening when, all of a sudden, I pulled over to the side of the road—for no reason. Surprised at myself for doing such a fool thing, I got out and walked around my car, then started to open the door again. But the door wouldn't budge." Excitement rose in his voice as he continued, "Just then I heard someone say, 'Don't get back in!' Well, I admit that gave me the willies, because no one else was there—just me! So I walked around a bit more until I happened to look down over the bank. There was just enough moonlight for me to spy what looked like an arm—*your* arm!"

Spider felt goose bumps sprout all over. He wondered, *Did this "Good Samaritan" really hear some supernatural voice?*

The policeman finished the story. "Dragging you up the bank, he loaded you into his car and brought you here. You were in pretty bad shape and would have died, the doctor said, if this fellow hadn't gotten you here when he did."

Spider again tried to speak, managing to express his appreciation with, "Thank you, sir!"

"Don't mention it!" The man gripped Spider's arm, then studied the patient a moment before speculating, "You know, I think there must be some reason the Lord wants you to stay alive, because I heard that voice as plain as day." With that pronouncement, he turned and walked out.

Suzy was the next to visit. When she saw her husband's swollen face and bruised arms, she could hardly hold back the tears.

"I'm sorry," he said, then launched into the story about his own personal Good Samaritan.

When he finished, Suzy smiled that same smile that caught so poignantly at his memory. "We should start going back to church," she told him.

Spider wriggled uncomfortably. "I'll think about it."

On May 16, 1967, Suzanne gave birth to another son, whom she named Michael. Spider's long convalescence and his obvious drinking habit brought an end to his trash collection job. Evicted from their rental house, the Monteros moved to a different Los Angeles neighborhood, that of Compton, where Spider's mother and the youngest children had migrated earlier after the death of his grandmother. Although Spider's father had wandered off again, at least his family had finally escaped the sad, burned-out community of Watts. And at his mother's request, Spider moved his own family into her Compton home, which shrank considerably with five more occupants.

The evening they settled in, Spider noted his wife's glum mood as she fed the baby. "Don't look so sad!" he said. "I'm feeling well again, strong enough to make good money. And we'll soon rent a place of our own, I promise."

Suzy then voiced her hope that he would give up riding with the gang, stop dealing in drugs, and settle down to a more "normal life." Instead, a few days later, her husband fell in with an even larger gang of motorcyclists based throughout Los Angeles.

On a hot July night, after Spider had been gone a long while with his new friends, Suzanne exploded when he finally stumbled into the house. "Where have you been?" she screamed.

"Shush! You'll wake my mom and the kids."

Suzy looked wild with worry and anger. "You think she could sleep? She's been afraid you were jumped again and maybe this time got your throat slit." Her voice trembled. "I can't take this anymore. We have three beautiful children you never see—except when you're too blind drunk to make any sense."

"Look who's talking!" he scoffed. "You drink just as much as I do."

She whirled around. "I'm leaving you, Spider. Everything's packed, and my brother's coming to take us to my stepmother's. She says she'll take us in till I can find a place of my own."

Spider retorted with a bitter laugh. "Oh, sure! You won't stay away long. You could never make it by yourself."

Suzy ignored him, and when her brother arrived, she herded the two older children out to the car. When she returned to scoop up Michael, Spider taunted, "You'll come back. You'll see. You can't do without me." Then they were gone, leaving Spider to brood alone in the empty living room.

After a couple of weeks, when Suzy and the children didn't return as expected, Spider sought out his family. On the pretense of giving them money for support, he asked to see the children. Suzy shrugged, letting him in. "Go ahead!"

The small tanned faces lit up at the sight of their father, and five-year-old Lydia ran straight into Spider's arms. He hugged her tightly and then talked with her about kindergarten, her grandma, and other things of interest to little girls. Robert, at three-and-a-half, acted a bit shy. But the toddler, Michael, grinned profusely and babbled nonstop, as if to report on the entire two weeks.

Playing with the baby, Spider stole a peak at his wife while she washed dishes. His heart stirred at the sight of her, the way her hair parted, half in front and half flowing down her back. Her beauty hadn't faded over the years, he noticed. In fact, she had grown even more beautiful in his eyes.

Upon leaving, he asked her, "Are you ready to come home?"

Suzy's forehead furrowed in question: "Are you ready to give up the gang and dealing?"

He threw some twenty-dollar bills at her feet, turned in a huff, then headed out the door for his bike. Who did she think she was anyway? Trying to tell *him* how to run his life—asking him to give up his closest friends, his soul mates who would stick by him through tough times and good! No woman, however beautiful, was going to tell him what to do.

After moving from his mother's place and into his own home in Compton, Spider visited Suzy and the children again. "I've got a nice little house rented for all of us," he told her excitedly. "Lydia would have her own room ..."

"And a decent job?" Suzy cut in, her voice hopeful.

"I've got a good job. Look!" He pulled out a roll of bills, slapping it down on the table. "You and the kids could live like kings on this kind of money."

"What kind of job, Spider?"

"I'm selling. What else?"

"Forget it!" she retorted. "I don't want our kids growing up around those cycle thugs and the danger that comes along with them."

Spider fought the desire to take her in his arms and admit how much he had missed her. But his *machismo* again intruded. "Will you at least keep the money?" he asked gruffly.

She nodded, sighing. "We have to live."

On the next visit, Spider found that Suzy and the children had moved out of her stepmother's place and were living a few blocks away. Again, he brought them funds. Again, he enjoyed a pleasant visit with the children. Again, he tried to coax Suzy back home.

But she remained firm in her resolve. "When you have an honest job and you're not hanging out with those cycle creeps anymore, we'll come back. Not until then."

"But, Suzy," he argued, pacing back and forth, "I could never make this kind of money driving some stupid truck or picking fruit or digging ditches. Better jobs take better schooling. And, anyway, I'm *Chicano*. Chicanos are supposed to stay in their place, you know. There are black people who have better jobs than Chicanos." Spider realized that Caesar Chavez was working toward improved employment for his Mexican-American *compadres*, but he also understood such change would take years. Besides, Spider knew how to make money, even if it was illegal. Once more, he left Suzy and the children behind and returned to his life of drug peddling and aimless partying with the motorcycle gang.

The image of Lydia's sad face, of her clinging to him when he left, pricked his conscience time and again. So did the memory of his small sons. "They're growing up without me," he thought disgustedly. At least he had had his grandfather's guidance when he was young—until he began breaking the old man's heart. He remembered the prediction made years ago: *I afraid someday you become like your father ... Your children, they grow up like you, with no father most of time.*

History was repeating itself, and Spider felt helplessly trapped by an invisible whirlpool. Pictures of his drunken parent, sprawled nightly on the couch, rushed to his mind, and he thought of the uncertain months of Henry Montero's absence when the family did not know his whereabouts or even whether he was alive. In his youth, Spider had vowed never to put his own family through such anguish. He had wanted to be there for his children when they needed his help. He had wanted to pass on to them the wisdom, talents, and proud heritage of his grandfather. But now, all those hopes were fast disappearing as the months passed and Spider remained separated from his family.

Sometimes, as he rode through a residential section of town, there would be couples frolicking with their children in yards, and the happy scenes seemed to squeeze the life from his very soul.

He tried to suppress his heartache with more alcohol and drugs. But that destructive combination sent him spiraling into another deep depression. He felt like such a failure in life that death began looking good to him. "Death can't be worse than this," he thought.

One night, while riding in the front seat of a friend's car as it sped down a highway, Spider grabbed the handle and pushed open the door, fighting against the wind.

"Hey, man!" his friend yelled when Spider thrust himself out of the car. He hoped to end his life on the hard asphalt or under the wheels of traffic. Instead, his body rolled to a harmless stop beside the road. He swore, picked himself up, and staggered back to where the car had pulled over.

His friend gasped. "I thought you'd be dead for sure."

Spider glowered at him. "I can't even kill myself right," he murmured, then asked, "Where's the whiskey?"

Not too long after that, Spider's motorcycle was pursued again, this time by an erratic car. "Ha!" he thought. "Either that guy's just plain mean or he's drunker 'n I am!"

Spider didn't even attempt to outrun the other vehicle. He let it shove his cycle off the road. And as he lay in the gravel face up, he listened to the car's motor thrum down a notch or two. It was turning around. Spider eyed the headlights closing in on him as the engine revved higher and higher.

He could easily have moved out of its path, but with a twisted grin, he hollered, "Come and get me, mister! I'm all yours." Clenching his teeth, he felt a tire roll over his chest. Then the taillights disappeared into the night.

Spider lay there stunned. His chest hurt somewhat, but not at all like he had expected. He tried his fingers and toes. Everything wiggled. Then he slowly rose to his feet and began to curse up at the black sky. "Why won't You let me die?" Angry tears coursed down his face as he recovered his wounded Harley and rode slowly home. *God won't even let me die. It's not fair.* He cursed some more.

In that moment, a memory of the ruddy-faced man who had saved Spider's life flashed to mind, when he had said, "There must be some reason the Lord wants you to stay alive." Was there some reason? Spider wondered. Some worthwhile reason—not just to punish him? Was there any chance Spider could make something of his life, restore his family, maybe even give up the drinking and drugs?

Then he remembered his terror-filled bout with the DTs. "Nah!" he concluded. He was hooked—for life. Spider could see no way out.

CHAPTER 10

SMOTHERING BLACK CLOUD

Because his several attempts at suicide had been fruitless, Spider gave up the idea for a while. But an oppressive black cloud continued to hover around him. No matter how much he drank, how far he rode, or how long he partied with the gang, that same smothering cloud of depression remained.

Eighteen months had passed since he and Suzanne had first separated. One afternoon, when Spider dropped by her place with the usual support money, a stubble-faced stranger greeted him. "Whatcha want?" he growled.

Spider was caught off guard. "To see my kids," he said calmly enough. But his heart was racing out of control. *Who is this man?* He dreaded the answer.

"They're all at her stepmom's," the stranger retorted, slamming the door.

Within minutes, Spider sat pensively listening while Suzy explained, "He's got a real job, he's nice to me and the kids, and he don't do drugs." Although her words sounded sympathetic, they were cutting his spirit to shreds, especially when she added, "He takes good care of us."

"But, Suzy, I want to take care of you." Spider's voice choked off. To spare himself any further humiliation, he left.

Hopping aboard the Harley, he rode directly uptown where he rented a hotel room in Los Angeles' skid-row district. Next, he visited the closest liquor store. Clutching one bag filled with all sorts of spirits and another chockfull of snack food, such as pretzels and chips, Spider invited every wino he met along the way to his room for a party.

Amid the noise and stench of unwashed vagrants, Spider drank. He drank to forget the beautiful face of his childhood bride who had chosen to live with another man. He drank to forget young Lydia, a second grader now, and his son, Robert, who was proud to be in kindergarten. He drank to forget Michael, who was no longer a baby.

The sun had set, and the single bare bulb strung above the dingy room barely lit the bearded and blotched faces around him. Some of the men had passed out on the floor. Some leaned, half-conscious, against the peeling wall. Every now and then, a bold cockroach would dart out of hiding and snatch up a stray crumb. The odor in the place had become intolerable, and even in his stupor, Spider could no longer stand the smell. Opening the unscreened window, he let in air from the alley behind the hotel. But the stale odor of rotting garbage wandered up to his nostrils. Spider sighed, and hoisting himself onto the windowsill, he took another long gulp of whiskey.

Again, thoughts of his beautiful Suzy in the arms of another man stabbed through his foggy mind. The black cloud was smothering, and he realized that all the alcohol in the world would never banish that awful oppressive feeling. He tottered on the sill, suddenly aware of his height above the concrete alley floor—two or three stories? He couldn't recall. But it was high enough to bring an end to his suffering. He couldn't live any longer without his Suzy and the kids, he thought.

Almost reverently, Spider set the whiskey bottle upright at his feet. "Here, fellows!" he blustered. "Drink and enjoy, 'cuz this is probably the only funeral I'll have." Then, rocking backward, he let himself fall freely through the air.

To Spider's shock, his landing was a soft one—atop two moldy mattresses apparently left for garbage collectors! He lay there, sprawled on the yellow-stained cotton, stunned at first. Then he began to laugh, a loud, uproarious, crazy-sounding laugh that ricocheted down the alley walls.

Afterward, he picked himself up and bounced down to ground level. This time, he didn't curse at God. Instead, he found his cycle and somehow made the way back to his Compton neighborhood where he slept long into the next day.

After showering, he donned his freshest shirt and pair of jeans. Then he tried to dredge up the courage to face Suzy by fortifying himself with whiskey.

That evening, he stood at her door and, surprisingly, she invited him in. "You been drinking?" she asked.

"Some."

"A lot, you mean." Offering him a seat on the couch, she lectured, "You shouldn't be driving when you've had so much booze."

Spider was nervously glancing around. "Where's what's-his-name?"

"What's-his-name is at work. He don't usually come home till about two or so in the morning."

"Daddy?" came a faint voice behind him.

"Lydia!" Spider exclaimed.

The girl wandered over and climbed onto his lap. "I have to go to bed now," she told him, "'cause I gotta get up early for school. Mike and Robert are already asleep."

Spider took her hand and tiptoed to the children's room, where he gazed at his sleeping sons. Then he tucked his daughter into her bed, kissed her forehead, and returned to the living room where Suzy was replacing his leather jacket on the couch.

"What're you doin'?" he asked suspiciously.

"I hid your keys so you won't drive until you've sobered up."

Spider chuckled. "I haven't been sober since I was ten or younger. You know that." Then his voice took on a more serious tone. "Suzy, I've got to talk to you, tell you all the crazy things that have happened to me lately." He began to relate his thwarted attempts at suicide, including his deliberate fall out of a hotel window the night before.

She gasped. "I can't believe it! Mattresses!" Then the couple enjoyed a hearty laugh together. But the smile quickly faded from Suzy's face when she confessed, "I'm glad those mattresses saved your neck, Spider. I don't want you to die. After all, why on earth would I hide your keys?" She didn't say she still loved him. But she did admit to feeling no hate.

Then Spider and Suzanne Montero began to talk—really talk—for the first time since those brief magical moments after Lydia's birth when the two had felt bonded somehow. They recalled the time they had met in the school hallway. They even reached way back into their pasts on San Carlos Apache Indian Reservation and shared the happy times each had experienced there before moving to Watts.

"I think that when my mother died, I was suddenly forced to grow up," Suzy said. "At six years old, I seemed to lose my childhood."

Spider nodded knowingly. "Yes, I lost mine somewhere along the way, too. With my father's problem and his taking off the way he did, Mary Ann and I had to grow up pretty fast and help my mother keep the family together." He peered earnestly into Suzy's dark eyes. "Children need to be children, don't you think? And you and me, we were robbed of that. Maybe that's why we've made such a mess of things as grownups, huh?"

As they continued their conversation, Spider felt something of promise and of healing steal between them. They talked on and on, never realizing the late hour—until they heard a key in the kitchen door.

In stalked Spider's rival. "I figured that was your bike out there," he said. "Now, get out of here!" he ordered in the thick speech of someone who had visited several bars on his way home.

When Spider stood to leave, Suzy stopped him. "If anyone has the right to stay here," she declared haughtily, "it's the father of my children." Spider suddenly acquired new respect for Suzanne as she stood toe-to-toe with the disgruntled figure that towered above her small frame. She further commanded, "*You* leave!" The man cast a hateful look at Spider before retreating.

When Suzy brought in a pillow and blanket for her guest to sleep on the couch, Spider asked, "Is there any chance you and me might get back together?" He caught the glimmer of a smile with her reply, "I think there's a chance."

The children were delighted to find their daddy at the breakfast table. Later, Spider walked Lydia and Robert to their bus stop before he boarded his cycle for the ride home. He felt a new surge of hope inside, a feeling he hadn't experienced for years. His Harley seemed to float back to the house, where Spider cleaned up and started on his promise to Suzy—to find an "honest job."

When he returned home that evening, his spirits still soared high. But a phone call changed things in an instant. Suzy's boyfriend had apparently gotten revenge by beating her into unconsciousness. Spider heard his stepmother-in-law's voice over the receiver, "She's in the hospital, and there ain't no use in your coming here, 'cuz she don't know nobody."

"The children?" Spider pleaded.

"They're okay. My daughter and I'll take care of 'em."

When the phone clicked off, Spider crumpled to the floor. His head was spinning, fighting off the horror of what had happened to his beloved Suzy. A whiskey bottle looked down on him from the kitchen table. He groped for it, but before it reached his lips, he threw it against the wall and watched the glass and liquid splatter.

Memories were flooding him, all the hurt his Suzy had suffered over the years—her mother dying, her sister's brutal slaying, the death of little Anthony—and now this, this terrible attack from someone who was "nice to her and the children," she had said. Spider sobbed until he retched. Then a rage boiled up, replacing his grief.

When another phone call came from his in-law, her voice choked on the horrific message: "The doctor said a blood clot ... her brain ... She's dead, Spider. Suzy is dead."

CHAPTER 11

RESPECTABLE ALCOHOLIC

There followed the darkest days of Spider Montero's life. Suzy, his childhood sweetheart, his bride, was dead. If it weren't for the tie with his children, Spider would have ended his life for sure during those black hours. The smothering blanket of depression had returned.

Spider couldn't sleep, and when he did, the bed held him like quicksand. Why get up? Why shave? Why shower? Why continue to look for an honest job? Suzy was gone, and nothing could ease his sorrow. He would lie in his disheveled bed for hours, stare up at the ceiling, and let the past wash over him, remembering. His last night together with Suzy, the closeness between them, the promise in her words, all those memories returned to taunt him. Time and again, he asked himself, "What could I have done so this terrible thing wouldn't have happened?"

His gang buddies tried to console Spider. But their chatter and jokes—even their awkward condolences—floated over him. And the liquor they brought barely dulled the emptiness he felt.

Coming so close to reuniting with his wife, then abruptly losing her, seemed to snuff out Spider's will to fight. But that will wasn't completely extinguished, he soon discovered, when his in-laws demanded custody of the children. In spite of his grief, he rose from his do-nothing existence and hired a lawyer. Then, after several months of battling the relatives in court, Spider at last won back Lydia, Robert, and Michael.

Suzanne's wish—however late—was finally realized when Spider left the motorcycle gang behind and carted his children north to Oregon. One of his sisters had moved there when she had wed a few years before.

As he drove through the mountains in the southern part of the state, Spider rolled down the window and drew in a deep breath. "Smell that fresh air, kids! Look at the scenery! Isn't it beautiful?"

"Uh-huh," agreed Lydia beside him.

"How much longer, Dad, till Aunt Mary's?" came Robert's weary voice from the back seat.

"I'm afraid Portland's a long ways yet." But he assured the children, "We'll camp someplace tonight and get to my sister's house by tomorrow."

Although the role as sole caretaker was new to Spider, his instincts told him to move his children far from their former environment and the harsh memories associated with it. He wanted to start over with a clean slate and act like the father Suzanne had begged him to be.

Spider's intentions were the best, but one major problem had followed him straight over the California border—his alcoholism. Whatever semblance of a normal life he grasped for himself and the children would always be threatened by his addiction to alcohol. He drank just enough to keep the DTs at a distance, but he still maintained his respectability. In fact, he jokingly termed himself "a respectable alcoholic."

In spite of the addiction, Spider was able to make opportunities work for him during that time. He trained in body and fender work and landed a good job in Southeast Portland. Soon afterward, he rented a tidy, four-bedroom house in a well-kept neighborhood that sprawled against a backdrop of low-lying, lush, green hills. Shopping at the better grocery and department stores, he kept his children well fed and suitably dressed.

For two years, Spider kept up the façade. Soon after Lydia's tenth birthday, however, he noticed an increase in his craving for alcohol and found himself drinking more, and more often. It was as if the "drink demon" had been toying with him all along, allowing Spider to dabble in the good life awhile, only to tighten the line suddenly. Now he felt a sharp hook in his very flesh, the awful craving that sent him back to a bottle with greater frequency.

One Sunday morning, his cozy, warm house echoed with children's laughter as he stared moodily out at the rain-washed hills. He was considering asking some agency—maybe even a priest—for help. No, he decided. They would take away his children and send them off to some strangers to raise, perhaps separating them. He couldn't take that chance. He would have to fight this battle alone, a battle he was already losing. To ease the intensified craving for alcohol, Spider had begun to use certain illegal drugs again.

No one at work seemed to suspect his habits, however, as he continued to handle his job with skill. For two years, he had gloried in his work as a "car doctor," taking unsightly, wounded automobiles and refashioning them into like-new models. He reveled in watching for smiles as customers inspected his handiwork. They were reminiscent of the smiles long ago when, under a ramada, visitors looked over his grandfather's wares. Instead of using his artistic talents to make impressions in metal, however, Spider removed any impressions from the metal and still brought joy into people's lives. He had felt deep satisfaction with the job, but now the combination of drugs and alcohol dampened any enthusiasm for his work.

The evening he dropped by a bar before heading home to the children was doomed at the onset. One drink turned to two, then four. By the time he found his car in the parking lot, he could hardly climb inside without toppling over.

A few blocks from the bar, Spider noticed flashing lights in his rear-view mirror, but he was too drunk to realize the depth of his troubles. The DWI (driving while intoxicated) charge resulted in the suspension of his license. Asking people for transportation to work threw his life into turmoil. Sometimes he obtained rides, sometimes he hitchhiked, and sometimes he simply stayed home and drank.

Spider could feel his life spiraling downward, but he didn't seem to have any control to stop it. He watched helplessly as Lydia assumed the role of parent for her younger siblings. She cooked, kept the house in passable order, and guided her brothers safely to the bus stop every weekday morning.

Oftentimes, Spider awoke long after the children had left for school, his head throbbing and his entire body screaming for a drink and his morning cigarette. When his employer's patience ran out, Spider abruptly joined the ranks of the unemployed. He felt terribly fatigued to the depths of his soul—and lonely. He longed for adult companionship, someone he could complain to, someone like himself who could nod understandingly, perhaps another Native American.

Finally, one day, soon after losing his job, Spider disregarded the order not to drive. Nursing his car engine to life, he headed downtown toward a bar where other jobless Indians hung out. But Spider never reached it. A patrol car intercepted, hauling him off to jail.

Bad then turned to worse for Spider Montero. In a short time, all the beautiful dreams he had had for his children had disintegrated. Just as he had dreaded, Lydia, Michael, and Robert were turned over to the state foster care system while their father began serving his first prison term. No sooner was he released than a second term followed for violation of parole—then a third term.

When Spider finally walked out of the Oregon State Penitentiary for the third time, he knew that his children were leaving their childhood behind—and to his regret, he had shared only a small portion of that time with them. His sister, Mary Magdalene, had been allowed to visit the children, and she had kept Spider up-to-date on their progress through elementary, middle, and now, high school.

During the hour's bus ride between Salem and Portland, Spider watched the fertile Willamette Valley roll past his window. Compared to the restricted space inside prison, the earth looked incredibly vast to him. There was something in his Native American spirit that savored the boundless views and the taste of freedom.

"I must never go back inside. I'll die first," he vowed to himself. He had wasted too many years and now was determined to walk a straight path, staying well within the parameters of his parole. With this chance at another fresh start, Spider hoped he might salvage some kind of relationship with his children. As an "ex-con," however, he realized he would have to wait patiently for all the children to emerge from the state care system before any genuine bonding as a family could take place. But one virtue Spider had surely nurtured throughout his years of imprisonment was patience.

Upon his arrival back in Portland, he set up housekeeping in a small, but adequate, downtown apartment. Picking up odd jobs here and there, he managed to support himself— and his revived drinking habit.

One late-summer evening, as Spider walked the city's balmy streets, he met an old buddy. After a friendly greeting, the fellow said, "I heard your PO (parole officer) has been hunting fer ya."

"What for? I been straight."

"I dunno. Just the word I got was your PO's gonna violate ya."

Without hesitating, Spider raced back to his apartment, packed his few belongings, then went out into the night to blend with the other aimless faces of Portland's street people. Within an hour, based on hearsay, Spider had thrown away his attempt at a new life and had taken on the harsh one of a downtown drifter. "But I'm staying out of the joint," he reasoned.

A long Indian summer stretched out the warm days that kept his nights fairly comfortable under a bridge or an overpass. Afternoons would find him lounging in a patch of sunlight, listening to the soothing waters of the Willamette River ripple against the bank. Even when autumn rains came, Spider continued to sleep outdoors.

But as impending winter began to chill the "City of Roses," he opted for a place in a flophouse at night. And he could usually eat at least one wholesome meal a day there if he stood in line long enough. It wasn't the best life, but at least he was free, he reminded himself.

One evening, a bitter wind gusted through an alley as Spider headed to what he hoped would be a meal and a warm bed for the night. On the way, he ran into another friend.

"What do ya say? Is it cold enough fer ya?"

Spider nodded. "Feels like it might snow."

"Well, I got an extra pint you can have," offered the man, who reached into his thrift-store overcoat and pulled out a bottle. "This'll warm ya right up."

"Thanks a million!" Spider exclaimed, grinning greedily at the gift. The air *was* cold, he mused, and the whiskey would at least make him *feel* warm. Shivering there in the deserted alley, he stared at the bottle, so beautifully labeled. Suddenly, the truth glared at him squarely in the face. The contents of that elegant-looking bottle had contributed to his loss of Suzy, his children, and even the roof over his head. It was the cause of years wasted in prison. He wondered how something so seemingly harmless could control him and cause such grief.

Then he heard a voice say, "You don't have to drink that. There are better things for you to do."

Startled, he called out, "Who's there?" searching the shadows around him. With goose bumps prickling his neckline, he realized he was alone. *Am I hearing things now? Have I crossed over into loco land?*

Reluctantly, he chucked the unopened bottle into a nearby trash bin, picked up his knapsack, and headed for a detox center.

"I wanna stay upstairs," he told the man who opened the door to him. Upstairs meant "drying out," which also meant another bout with the dreaded DTs. But Spider gritted his teeth and faced the several-day ordeal. At least in the detox center he would get medical help and a well-padded room where he couldn't bruise himself.

He survived the tremors, the hallucinations, and the indescribable terror. Afterward, Spider was sent to NARA (Native American Rehabilitation Association).

Checking in, he found his room and stashed his few, freshly laundered clothes in a drawer. Feeling somewhat apprehensive, he ambled back downstairs to an office. There he met the warm grin of Rod, his counselor, who was a fellow American Indian.

Rod made Spider feel comfortable at once and began to ask him probing questions. In time, the whole ugly story unraveled: his father's alcoholism, his own early alcohol abuse, the gang activities, the murder of Suzy's sister, the death of little Anthony, his relationship with motorcycle gangs, the hit-and-run, his brushes with death, the drug peddling, the separation from Suzy, then her brutal beating and subsequent death.

When Spider finished, he and Rod sat silently across from each other for long moments before the counselor's pensive voice broke the spell. "I want you to take this pen and paper up to your room and write a letter to your wife."

"But Suzy's dead," Spider protested.

"I know that, but I believe you haven't let her go. I think that's connected somehow to the root of your continuous drinking problem." Rod handed a tablet and pen to Spider, saying, "If Suzy *were* still alive, and you got the chance to make things up to her, what would you say? Write those things—all you can think of—on paper. Pour out your soul to her, as if she could actually receive the letter."

Spider felt uneasy. "Uh, I don't write so good."

"That's okay. You'll know what it says."

Baffled by what he thought a ridiculous request, Spider climbed the steps to the hallway where his bedroom waited. Still feeling foolish, he sprawled on the mattress and began to write:

My dear Suzy,

I have missed you so, so much. Oh, if I had the chance again, I would leave the booze and drugs alone. I would make you and the kids happy. I would work at an honest job, not ride with the gang. Please, I beg of you, forgive me.

The message ran on and on. He spoke of her beauty, of his devotion to her, of his regret. He soon felt tears soaking his face, and then watched them drop to the paper, splotching the ink. When he finally finished the letter, his entire body felt wrung of all strength. The pen weighed heavily in his hand. Still, a new sense of freedom was rising within him. It was a good feeling, something akin to racing his motorcycle through the wild countryside on a warm, spring day.

He gathered the papers, read them again, then returned to Rod's office where the counselor helped Spider destroy the letter.

Next Rod said, "I want you to go back up to your room and do whatever comes to your mind."

Frankly puzzled, Spider shrugged, but made the climb up the stairs again. *Whatever comes to your mind …?*

CHAPTER 12

RADICAL REDEMPTION

Spider leaned against the closed door and glanced around at the sparsely furnished room. Rod had mentioned a "Higher Power" to him earlier and said that only that "Power" could restore him and make his life manageable, that Spider on his own could never overcome his addictions to alcohol and drugs.

At the time, those words had slapped at Spider's pride, and the old *machismo* bristled angrily within him. After all, he had survived gang wars, even worse over the years, using his own cunning and strength. Spider Montero was a self-made man and almost arrogant about it.

Upon deeper reflection, however, he sank onto the bed and admitted to one war he had never been able to win on his own—his lifelong battle with alcohol. At an early age, he had given in and allowed the substance to control him, and it had ever since, leading him down dark and lonely paths.

Again, he focused on Rod's advice. "That Higher Power is God," Spider mumbled to himself. His concept of God was a unique one, an odd mix based upon his Roman Catholic upbringing and the deep spiritualistic roots of his Indian ancestry. But Spider did believe in God's existence. He knew that only a being much greater than any human could have saved him from certain death so many times. Those weren't mere coincidences, he realized. And what about the voice in the alley? He wondered if that was God speaking or, at least, one of His angels.

Spider hadn't seriously prayed since his altar-boy days at the church in the barrio. He glanced around again at his simple bedroom. It was far different from the decorative sanctuary where he had worshipped as a child. Nor was there any priest to confess to here. Nonetheless, he knelt down beside the bed and invited God to hear him—"please."

As before, Spider felt a bit silly, but still basking in the pleasant results of the letter to Suzy, he decided to go ahead and stumble through some type of prayer. "Forgive me, Father, for I have sinned." He recited the familiar words from his confessional days. Then, one by one, he confessed his wrongs. It was as if he were unloading a heavy bag of ugly, cancerous tumors and, at the same time, becoming lighter and healthier in the process.

After what seemed like hours, he finally faced his fear of the future. What good would all this cleansing do if he fell back into his old habits? Other doubts assailed him, like, could he make it in the world without his longtime crutches of alcohol and drugs? Could he even live with his own personality after keeping it dulled and buried for so long?

He drew in a deep breath and spat out the words, "Father, take the alcohol! Take the drugs! I don't need them." In that instant, something unexplainable happened inside, and he grew excited. "Yes, and take everything, God! I want for me only what *You* want for me."

Without realizing it, in his own clumsy way, Spider Montero had just experienced several of the Twelve Steps in the Alcoholics Anonymous (AA) program. Later, with others at AA meetings, he would discuss and work through all of those steps:

1. We admitted we were powerless over alcohol—that our lives had become unmanageable.

2. Came to believe that a Power greater than ourselves could restore us to sanity.

3. Made a decision to turn our will and our lives over to the care of God *as we understood Him*.

4. Made a searching and fearless moral inventory of ourselves.

5. Admitted to God, to ourselves, and to another human being the exact nature of our wrongs.

6. Were entirely ready to have God remove all these defects of character.

7. Humbly asked Him to remove our shortcomings.

8. Made a list of all persons we had harmed and became willing to make amends to them all.

9. Made direct amends to such people wherever possible, except when to do so would injure them or others.

10. Continued to take personal inventory and when we were wrong promptly admitted it.

11. Sought through prayer and meditation to improve our conscious contact with God *as we understood Him*, praying only for knowledge of His will for us and the power to carry that out.

12. Having had a spiritual awakening as the result of these Steps, we tried to carry this message to alcoholics and to practice these principles in all our affairs.

Spider also attended daily classes and group therapy sessions at NARA, interacting with others who had traveled many of the same roads as he. During that time of deep and earnest soul-searching, Spider began to express his feelings in the form of poetry. The following described how he saw life when he was consumed by alcohol and drugs:

THE SINKING SOUL

by Spider Montero

Look at your heart; has love turned it cold?

So bitter the kiss to the body that sold.

Respect is lost as you walk the street,

From booze to drugs, we all claim defeat.

Tears in my eyes as I recall the past

Of what I would have if the drugs didn't last.

I reached out for help, yet no help was there,

So my life sank down till I fell into despair.

No cash could buy all that I've lost,

All the heartaches and tears,

For them, there's no cost.

So, look at your heart; has love turned it cold?

So bitter the kiss to the body that sold.

His poetic creations weren't all so woeful. Another revealed a more optimistic perspective:

LOOKING ON THE SUNNY SIDE

by Spider Montero

There are always two sides, the good and the bad,

The dark and the light, the safe and the glad.

But in looking over the good and the bad,

We're aware of the number of good things we've had.

And in counting our blessings, we

find when we're through

We've no reason at all to complain or be blue.

So thank God for the good things He has already done.
And be grateful to Him for the battles you've won.
And know that the same God who helped you before
Is ready and willing to help you once more.
Then with faith in your heart, reach out for God's hand
And accept what He sends, though
you can't understand.
For our Father in Heaven always knows what is best,
And if you trust in His wisdom,
your life will be blessed.
For always remember that whatever betides you,
You are never alone, for God is beside you.

During the long months of rehabilitation at NARA, Spider's world began to change. Colors seemed more vivid. The trees, the grass, even the aged brick looked varnished with some magic luster nature provided. He noticed sweet aromas filling the air and heard music where there was none before. It was as if he had suddenly awakened after years of sleep to a world refreshed, and how exquisite it was!

His childhood love of nature from reservation days returned to him with the bird's trill and squirrel's chatter in a nearby park.

There was still much to learn, amends to make, and others to help. Part of his recovery program involved reaching out to his children. He quickly discovered, however, that Lydia (now grown and on her own) had moved out of state and would be unreachable for a while. But Spider was able to contact his sons, and their first reunion was an emotional one.

Because his boys had become men during the years apart, he barely recognized the tall, handsome figures before him. In time, though, he saw Suzy in Robert's glance and heard her in Michael's speech, and he sensed his own iron will in them both.

Spider yearned to teach them the things he had taken four decades to learn. He wanted to shield them from the pain they would suffer if they made the same choices he had. Wisely, the father kept his counsel for the future, for small sprinklings of it as their lives would eventually intertwine.

At long last, Spider ventured a little ways from the shelter of NARA by obtaining part-time employment in Portland. One morning, Robert and Michael dropped by the market where their dad worked. The younger son informed him, "Robert and me, we're driving to Idaho to find a job. You wanna come, too?"

Spider thanked them for the offer, but admitted, "I'm still too new at this straight life. I'd better not fly very far from the nest just yet." Then he said, "Maybe later I'll go on over to Idaho and join ya." His departing sons promised to keep in touch.

In the meantime, upon Rod's advice, Spider began to hunt for a church. After exploring certain Bible passages for himself, he had become convinced that finding a church home was not only a directive from Heaven, but also a sure way to keep him on the road to recovery.

Still sporting his headband, longish hair, numerous tattoos, and Bohemian-style clothes, Spider tried several different denominations. Whatever church he visited, his appearance brought curious stares and, sometimes, outright snubs. Nothing seemed to daunt him, though. Compared to knife-wielding gangsters in dark alleys, those powdered and impeccably coiffed churchgoers looked harmless to him.

With the help of the religious services and his own personal Bible study, he was beginning to understand what Jesus Christ had done for him, Spider Montero, nearly two thousand years before. He was reading John's gospel, finding there a very friendly, openhearted Jesus. Spider marveled at His unlimited love, a love that had cost Jesus His life.

After a few more months, Spider had gained enough confidence to join his sons in Idaho. There his search for a church continued. And one day, he ventured up the steps of a small-town sanctuary. Glancing nervously around at all the conventional types filling the pews, Spider felt out of place and decided to leave. On his way through the door, however, a gentle hand touched his arm.

There stood a smiling elderly woman. "Please, don't go!" she urged. "Come back in and join us!"

Spider did. And later, while enjoying a fellowship picnic after services, he chatted with a "Pastor Dan," who himself had once ridden with a motorcycle club on the East Coast.

Feeling a rapport with the minister, Spider continued to show up at his services, and after some time, Pastor Dan invited him to special Bible meetings in a nearby town.

One evening, when the evangelist asked for testimonies, Spider shared his story with the congregation, ending with, "I still have to pray for strength every morning. I admit that I'm powerless without God. Only as I turn my will over to Him can He get me through each day."

Soon Spider was studying his Bible even more fervently as he prepared for baptism. Then, on his forty-sixth birthday in the summer of 1989, despite the black, stormy clouds threatening overhead, Spider Montero stood in an outdoor water tank while his good friend, Pastor Dan, pronounced the words, "I baptize you in the name of the Father, and of the Son, and of the Holy Spirit. Amen!"

Just as Spider came back up out of the water, the angry clouds parted, letting the sun shine warmly down on him. It was like a sign from Heaven, promising that his every sin was truly forgiven and all heartache and darkness was burned away by the Light of the World, Jesus. And now, Spider Montero could finally face a future brightened by something he had lacked all his life—*hope*!

EPILOGUE

Not long after Spider's baptism, he became involved with a nondenominational Christian motorcycle club, its home church based in Eastern Washington. Under a mentor, Preacher Mike, Spider studied hard for two years before receiving a special patch that qualified him to join other club members on "runs." These runs have taken him all over the United States, where he and the others minister at cycle convocations, including the annual rally at Sturgis, South Dakota; at camp meetings; and at various churches. They also testify at Alcoholics Anonymous (AA) meetings.

After another two years into this unusual ministry, Spider was licensed to preach. But ten more years would pass before Preacher Mike decided that Spider was ready for ordination. That sacred service in 2003 was Preacher Mike's last official act before he succumbed to cancer.

In the spring of 1995, then officially known as "Preacher Spider," he remarried. Debbie, his recently baptized bride, rode to the outdoor altar on—what else?—the best man's motorcycle. Two *Debbies* were married during that ceremony, one to a "Spider" and one to a "Grasshopper"! (Nicknames abound in motorcycle clubs, even in Christian ones.)

Debbie proved to be a healing force between Spider and his father Henry. After Spider's mother died, Henry felt her loss keenly. To encourage the lonely parent, Spider and Debbie hopped aboard their Harley and rode to Western Oregon. There, they took Henry to a barber for a haircut, then to a restaurant for a hearty brunch. Their last stop was at the cemetery where Spider's mom was buried. Standing beside her grave, Spider was astonished to hear his father praying.

Later, Henry opened up to Debbie, sharing his life's story with her, helping Spider to fill large gaps in his memories of the man who was more a stranger than a father throughout those growing-up years. At the same time, any resentment or pain melted away as the two men began to bond.

A few years later, Spider again boarded his cycle, this time heading to an Oregon hospital. Henry Montero had suffered a stroke, and Spider remained at his dad's bedside for three days and nights. During those long hours, Henry's other children and grandchildren visited the old patriarch who was comatose most of the time.

Although Spider doubted his father could hear him, he still shared in a gentle, quiet way about Jesus' incredible love and power to forgive. Then Spider whispered, "Dad, I love ya!" To his surprise, Henry replied, "Yes!" A lone tear, trickling down the well-worn face, gave Spider assurance of his father's salvation—and of their eventual reunion. The third evening, just before midnight, Henry Montero died.

Spider is the first to admit that his ministry is far from conventional. His bandanna or Indian headband over longish hair, his multiple tattoos and odd clothing might draw stares and frowns in regular churches. But he fits right in with the "outcasts" to whom he ministers. They listen to him about how God can provide the power daily to overcome addictions to alcohol and drugs. And many have been converted as a result.

No matter where his missions take him, Spider tries to attend church every weekend. He shares his testimony with whomever will listen and distributes Christian literature wherever he and his Harley travel.

While sharing his testimony at a special meeting in Eastern Oregon, Preacher Spider was reunited with an old friend, Jim, and his wife, Bertie. Jim confesses to once being one of the frowners, one of the holier-than-thou folks in conventional church pews, looking down his nose at struggling alcoholics and drug addicts. Then he noticed how sincere these people were in their craving for freedom from addictions. As Jim witnessed their tears and heard their desperate prayers, God peeled the blinders from the eyes of this longtime Christian; his attitude made a seismic shift until he and Bertie became deeply involved in helping addicts—Christian style! Amusingly, Jim became known as their "recovering Pharisee."

Spider recently endured chemotherapy and is now disease-free after months of treatment and convalescence. He's back on his Harley and praises God for giving him more time to tell his miraculous story—and to share the simple steps to Jesus with anyone the Holy Spirit sends his way.

ABOUT THE AUTHOR

Paula Montgomery lives with her logger-husband, Lee, on a mountain in Washington State. Their lives and those of their two children are depicted in her Becka Bailey book series, currently in its second printing: *Coyotes in the Wind*, *Down the River Road*, *A Summer to Grow On*, and *When November Comes*. (After their children graduated from college and the daughter was well situated in medical school, the author herself returned to college at the age of forty-eight, and two years later, she graduated with a BA in English and a minor in journalism.) Also in a second printing is Mrs. Montgomery's Hazel Weston Series, the true story of a girl growing up in Oregon long ago: *Canyon Girl*, *Valley Girl*, *Hood River Girl*, and *In Grandma's Footsteps*.

Today, the Montgomery children are married and—along with their respective spouses—serve communities in Tennessee and Oregon. In addition to writing, Paula Montgomery has recently launched another career, that of a nanny to her one-and-only grandchild who, she claims, already exhibits signs of becoming a best-selling author someday.